DATE DUE

DEMCO 38-296

GREAT WRITERS OF THE ENGLISH LANGUAGE

Writers of Mystery and Suspense

STAFF CREDITS

Executive Editor
Reg Wright

Series Editor
Sue Lyon

Editors
Jude Welton
Sylvia Goulding

Deputy Editors
Alice Peebles
Theresa Donaghey

Features Editors
Geraldine McCaughrean
Emma Foa
Ian Chilvers

Art Editors
Kate Sprawson
Jonathan Alden
Helen James

Designers
Simon Wilder
Frank Landamore

Senior Picture Researchers
Julia Hanson
Vanessa Fletcher
Georgina Barker

Picture Clerk
Vanessa Cawley

Production Controllers
Judy Binning
Tom Helsby

Editorial Secretaries
Fiona Bowser
Sylvia Osborne

Managing Editor
Alan Ross

Editorial Consultant
Maggi McCormick

Publishing Manager
Robert Paulley

Reference Edition Published 1989
Published by Marshall Cavendish Corporation
147 West Merrick Road
Freeport, Long Island
N.Y. 11520

Typeset by Litho Link Ltd., Welshpool
Printed and Bound in Italy by
L.E.G.O. S.p.a. Vicenza

LIBRARY OF CONGRESS
Library of Congress Cataloging-in-Publication Data
Great Writers of the English Language
         p. cm.
     Includes index vol.
     ISBN 1-85435-000-5 (set): $399.95
     1. English literature — History and criticism. 2. English
literature — Stories, plots, etc. 3. American literature — History
and criticism. 4. American literature — Stories, plots, etc.
5. Authors. English — Biography. 6. Authors. American — Biography.
I. Marshall Cavendish Corporation.
PR85.G66 1989
820'.9 – dc19   88-21077
                                                                          CIP

ISBN 1–85435–000–5 (set)
ISBN 1–85435–012–9 (vol)

GREAT WRITERS OF THE ENGLISH LANGUAGE

Writers of Mystery and Suspense

Mary Shelley

Edgar Allan Poe

Wilkie Collins

Arthur Conan Doyle

MARSHALL CAVENDISH · NEW YORK · TORONTO · LONDON · SYDNEY

CONTENTS

MARY SHELLEY

⇀ *1797-1851* ↼

Remembered today as the daughter of illustrious parents and the wife of a famous poet, Mary Shelley shrank from any form of publicity and contributed to the obscurity that still clouds her name. Many people are astonished to learn that as a quiet, intellectual girl of 19, she wrote one of the most imaginative and horrific novels of the time – *Frankenstein*. Mary's eight years with Shelley were marked by tragedy, trauma and exile, but they were also years of inspiration for her own distinctive imagination.

The Shadow of Fame

Drawn into an illustrious circle and a life of extraordinary intensity, Mary Shelley suffered more than her fair share of tragedy. Within a few years of a teenage elopement, she was widowed and alone.

Mary Shelley's life was overshadowed by her famous parents and husband. It was also overshadowed by the deaths of those she loved. She was born on 30 August 1797 to the pioneer feminist Mary Wollstonecraft and the political philosopher William Godwin. But Mary was never to know her mother. She died of septicaemia just 10 days after the birth, leaving Mary forever deprived of a secure, loving relationship.

Although Mary adored her father, he had little time to spend with her. He remarried a few years later and Mary took an immediate (and understandable) dislike to her new mother, Mrs Mary Jane Clairmont, an unremarkable but pretentious widow with two children, Charles and Jane. As she grew up, Mary Godwin took refuge in the studies which were to serve as a great consolation throughout her life.

SECRET AFFAIR

In 1812, when Mary was staying with a family friend near Dundee, a young and fervent admirer of Mary's father began to frequent the Godwin household. The visitor was Percy Bysshe Shelley, aristocrat, political revolutionary and poet, who was also highly imaginative, somewhat unstable and, to many women, irresistible. He had married at 19 and had a daughter, Eliza Ianthe. These details, however, did not stop him from falling for the 16-year-old Mary when she finally returned from Scotland in the spring of 1814. Mary was not strikingly attractive, but, according to a friend, she was 'agreeable, vivacious and sparkling, very pretty with fair hair and complexion and clear bright white skin' – and she was an intellectual.

For Shelley, now disillusioned with his young wife Harriet, Mary's attraction was all the greater because her parents were the remarkable William Godwin and Mary Wollstonecraft. By the end of June – after a clandestine courtship at Mary Wollstonecraft's grave – Shelley and Mary had declared their mutual love.

Godwin was horrified. He tried to persuade Shelley to patch up his relationship with Harriet, who was pregnant again, and insisted that he stopped seeing Mary. But he could not keep the lovers apart and at the end of July they decided to elope to the Continent. At the last moment they agreed that Mary's stepsister Jane – soon to adopt the name Claire – should come with them. Claire, with her dark hair, olive skin, exuberant and demanding nature, was in many ways the opposite of Mary, and Mary would soon regret the invitation.

The three young people fled to France and embarked on a journey through a country ravaged by war and starvation. Their high spirits carried them through but by the time they reached Switzerland, these, as well as their finances, had begun to wane. Mary was pregnant, unwell and irritated by Claire's company. Des-

Mary Shelley
A supposed portrait of the writer when she was 19. By now Mary had enjoyed a passionate, clandestine love affair with Shelley, who was married to another; had eloped with him against her father's and his family's wishes; had travelled to Switzerland and back with him; had watched him go into hiding to avoid imprisonment for debt; had given birth to a baby daughter by him and suffered the anguish of seeing her baby die just two weeks later.

Shelley Musuem, Bournemouth

Detail from the portrait by Pickersgill. National Portrait Gallery

The Bridge & Castle of Taymouth by A. Nasmyth. Fine Art Photographic Library

Illustrious father

(above) William Godwin was a radical intellectual who attracted a coterie of distinguished admirers. He had published a seminal work entitled An Enquiry Concerning Political Justice *and challenged contemporary thinking on politics and religion, as well as marriage. Despite his emancipated ideas, he was a distinctly selfish man who caused incalculable distress to his daughter.*

River Tay, Scotland

Frail and unwell, Mary, aged 14, was despatched to her father's friend William Baxter, near Dundee. She spent two happy years there, going for long walks on the Sidlaw hills and along the river Tay (left). As she wrote in her introduction to Frankenstein, *'It was beneath the trees of the grounds belonging to our [the Baxters'] house . . . that my true compositions, the airy flights of my imagination, were born and fostered.'*

perately short of money, the three decided, quite suddenly, to return home.

The problems, however, continued in England. Despite constant visits to banks, lawyers and moneylenders, Shelley had to go into hiding to avoid the bailiffs and the dreaded debtors' prison, leaving a pregnant Mary, terrified and alone. Eventually, Shelley succeeded in securing a loan, whereupon Mary's father, who was still hostile to the couple, made the first of a series of demands for money which were to plague Mary and Shelley throughout their life together.

In February 1815, when she was not quite seven months pregnant, Mary gave birth to a tiny, fragile daughter. Two weeks later she awoke to find that her baby had died. She desperately needed Shelley's support, but he was now more interested in her stepsister Claire, and left Mary to be comforted by an old university friend of his, Thomas Hogg. An entry in her journal reflects the anguish she felt over her loss: 'Dream that my little baby came to life again; that it had only been cold, and that we rubbed it before the fire and it lived.'

Gradually, Mary began to recover her good spirits, helped no doubt by Shelley's agreement that Claire should leave their household and by a financial settlement which guaranteed Shelley an annual income of £1000. They moved into a house on Bishopsgate Heath, at the edge of Windsor Forest, and Mary, who was pregnant again, happily settled into a private life with Shelley, in which they studied, wrote, walked and rowed on the Thames with friends. She developed from an ill, anxious girl into a confident young woman, and in January 1816 she gave birth to a strong, healthy son whom they named William after her father.

Childhood home

(above) Mary grew up in the modest surroundings of London's Skinner Street in Holborn. It was here, over a shop at number 41, that her parents lived, and here that she first set eyes on the ardent young poet and radical, Percy Bysshe Shelley.

Key Dates

1797 born in London

1814 elopes with Shelley

1816 William born; Fanny and Harriet commit suicide

1817 Clara born

1818 *Frankenstein* published; Clara dies

1819 William dies; Percy Florence born

1822 Shelley dies

1826 *The Last Man* published

1839 Shelley's *Poetical Works* published

1845 son Percy inherits

1851 dies in London

they heard that Shelley's wife Harriet had also committed suicide, by drowning herself in the Serpentine in Hyde Park. Shelley immediately set off for London to claim custody of his two children, Ianthe and Charles, and decided that he would have a better chance of doing so if he and Mary married. It was against his principles, but the ceremony duly took place in December 1816.

In January Claire, who was again living with the Shelleys, gave birth to a daughter, Allegra, and the chancery suit for custody of Shelley's children began. The following month, Mary realized she was pregnant again and they moved to Marlow in Buckinghamshire where she settled down to finishing *Frankenstein*.

In September she gave birth to a baby daughter Clara, but immediately succumbed to post-natal depression. At the same time Shelley's health – frequently bad – deteriorated drastically. In the meantime, there was a flurry of local speculation about Allegra's origins. Claire had never publicly explained her daughter's parentage but had always hoped that Byron would give his daughter a privileged upbringing. Gossip now put the Shelleys under pressure to help her.

In March 1818, they set off for Italy. The lively, affectionate Allegra was sent with their nursemaid, Elise, to Venice, and the rest of the party travelled to Tuscany. Meanwhile *Frankenstein* had been published anonymously and an excited Mary was beginning to get favourable reports about it.

In August, Shelley and Claire set out to see Allegra and ten days later Mary received a letter asking her to join them. Her daughter Clara, not yet one year old, was ill, but Mary felt that she must go. So began a

Meanwhile, Claire had succeeded in 'capturing' no less a figure than the poet Lord Byron. It was a brief affair, but by the time Byron departed for Switzerland, Claire was pregnant. Shelley and Mary, distressed by Godwin's continual demands for money, the public's indifference to Shelley's poems and their own rejection by society, were contemplating a return to the Continent, and Claire easily persuaded them to take her with them to Switzerland. Mary had been introduced to Byron and, while repelled by his excesses, had found him fascinating, and was happy to meet him again. Once more, the threesome travelled across the Continent and joined Byron, in May 1816, on the shores of Lake Geneva. Here they rented two adjacent villas and spent much time together, going on boating trips and talking long into the night at Byron's Villa Diodati. The conversation frequently turned to subjects of horror and one night they decided to make up ghost stories. This was the starting-point of Mary's first novel, *Frankenstein*.

Relations between the two households were strained, Byron having long lost interest in Claire. And as the summer came to an end, Mary and Shelley decided it was time to leave, and in September they arrived back in England.

UNFORESEEN TRAGEDIES
They settled in Bath, in happy domesticity, until they received the news that Mary's half-sister Fanny had committed suicide. Mary, stricken with guilt and grief, was almost expecting the next blow when in December

Graveside romance
(above) In order to escape the constant wranglings at home, and also to conduct her courtship in secret, Mary began meeting Shelley by her mother's grave in St Pancras Churchyard. It was here that, united in hearts and spirit, they declared their mutual love.

nightmare journey across Italy in which Mary had to watch her small daughter visibly failing in her arms. On arrival in Venice the baby died. In her anguish, Mary blamed Shelley for Clara's death and never fully forgave him.

A BLEAK WINTER

Mary, Shelley and Claire soon embarked on another period of travel, this time to Rome and Naples. Here they immersed themselves in the study of Italian and classical literature, but it was a bleak winter in which they all felt depressed and homesick. In February 1819, the birth of a girl named Elena Adelaide Shelley was registered in Naples. Her official parents were Mary and Shelley. But her true parentage has remained a source of speculation to this day. There have been claims that she was the daughter of Shelley and Claire, but more probably her parents were Allegra's nurse-maid Elise and Byron. Whoever they were, Elena was left with foster parents when the Shelleys once more returned to Rome.

Rome was Mary's favourite city, but she could not shake off a sense of gloom. Then, her beloved son William succumbed to a bout of dysentery. He seemed to rally, but suddenly, just two weeks after the first signs of illness, he died before Mary and Shelley's despairing and disbelieving eyes.

William's death was a blow which was to mark Mary for life. Quite unconsoled by the knowledge that she was pregnant again, she left Rome as quickly as she could and returned with the others to Tuscany. After five years of trouble and tragedy, Mary was in the

MARY WOLLSTONECRAFT

Detail from the portrait by Opie. National Portrait Gallery

Born in London in 1759, Mary Shelley's mother, Mary Wollstonecraft, experienced a difficult childhood. One of three daughters, she had little formal education and often witnessed her drunken father beating her mother. These scenes planted in her a determination to fight for the cause of women, to ensure, among other things, that girls received a decent education, that they had the possibility of supporting themselves and that they were not always physically and economically at the mercy of men. She wrote a book called *Thoughts on the Education of Daughters* and gradually found herself part of a distinguished and radical social circle. In 1792 she published *A Vindication of the Rights of Woman,* a pioneering feminist work which has recently been reprinted.

Her private life was less successful. At 32 she became infatuated with the painter Henry Fuseli and, reeling from that hopeless relationship, she travelled alone to France where she soon became involved with an American adventurer, Gilbert Imlay, and found herself pregnant by him. By the time their daughter Fanny was born in 1794, Imlay had already begun to tire of her. Mary attempted suicide, first in Paris, then in London, and it was not until she formed a friendship with William Godwin that she found genuine happiness. In March 1797 they married – Mary was pregnant. But their joy was to be short-lived – on 10 September 1797 Mary died a few days after giving birth to a daughter, Mary.

By Courtesy of Schillay & Rehs. Inc. New York. Fine Art Photographic Library

Alpine travels
Claire Clairmont (inset left), Mary's stepsister, joined the young lovers when they eloped to Switzerland and became increasingly unwelcome as their journey progressed. At a certain point Shelley invested in a donkey to help transport Mary and some of their belongings along the way. But the animal was tiny, ill and feeble and Shelley ended up by carrying it clasped to his bosom, with Mary and Claire following, exhausted, at the rear.

Percy Bysshe Shelley
(right) Poet, free-thinker and political revolutionary, Shelley swiftly captured Mary's heart. At 16, months after meeting him, she wrote the verse: 'But ah! I feel in this was given/ A blessing never meant for me,/ Thou art too like a dream from heaven/ For earthly love to merit thee!'

Detail from the painting by Severn. Memorial House, Rome/Scala

Fact or Fiction

ANOTHER WILLIAM

An alert and happy child, little William (named after Mary's father) was his parents' pride and joy. Mary felt a special closeness to him, but always had a sense of impending doom.

On one occasion, as her son lay sleeping in his cot, she wrote of another – fictional – William "with sweet laughing blue eyes" whose life is cruelly cut short. Her dark imagination pictured this boy "rosy with health" strangled by Frankenstein's monster. Her vision of death was prophetic. Three years later her own William fell ill with dysentery and died.

Field House

(right) Situated in the village of Warnham, near Horsham, Sussex, Shelley's family home reflected the luxury into which he was born. Quarrels with his father, however, kept Shelley away from the house for much of his life. Even when his grandfather died, Sir Timothy would not let him in to hear the reading of the will; Shelley reputedly sat on the steps in front of the house reading Milton's Comus.

In 1844, after old Sir Timothy's death, Mary's son Percy inherited the baronetcy and moved into the family residence, reclaiming what his father had been denied.

British Museum

throes of an emotional breakdown. Shelley offered her love and care, but she felt incapable of responding.

A son, Percy Florence, was born in November 1819, but Mary doubted that he would flourish and live. It was a difficult time for her. Godwin was demanding money again; Byron was refusing all Claire's pleas to let Allegra spend some time with her; and things were reaching breaking point between the two sisters. On top of this, Paolo Foggi, an ex-servant and husband of Elise, was attempting to blackmail them over little Elena Adelaide Shelley, who had recently died.

The only alleviation in Mary's difficulties came when Claire departed from the household and Mary was able to establish a happy working routine, writing her third novel *Valperga*. At the end of October 1820 the Shelleys moved to Pisa and made a number of new friends, including Edward and Jane Williams. Byron joined them a year later, having left Allegra behind in a convent, and shortly afterwards Edward John Trelawny, a swashbuckling adventurer, also arrived. He fuelled Shelley's love of water and boats with his tales of adventures at sea.

'EXPECTATION OF EVIL'

In some ways it was a happy time for Mary, until news came of Allegra's death from typhus. A distraught Claire joined them as they and the Williamses moved to a house on the Bay of Spezia. Mary was pregnant again and unwell, and while Shelley and Edward Williams threw themselves into the enjoyment of sailing their new boat, she began to feel depressed and inexplicably anxious.

In June she suffered a miscarriage. She was still weak from it when Shelley announced that he and Williams were going to sail up the coast to Leghorn. Years later she wrote that 'a vague expectation of evil shook me to agony' and she tearfully begged him not to go.

Both she and Jane Williams, with whom Shelley was now in love, received letters describing his and Will-

Funeral pyre

Edward Trelawny, deeply moved by the death of his friends, Shelley and Edward Williams, battled with the Italian authorities for permission to cremate Shelley in the style of his beloved Greeks. Having seemingly moved heaven and earth to do so, he finally won his concession and accordingly set up a funeral pyre in a wild and beautiful spot on the shores close to Via Reggio, near Florence. In classical Greek fashion, Trelawny procured salt and frankincense to fan the flames and poured wine and oil over the body. A copy of Keats' last book, which had washed ashore with Shelley, had been placed beside his body – so that the souls of the two great poets might, at some level, be merged together.

As the flames lapped Shelley's body, Trelawny plunged his hand into the fire and pulled out his friend's heart, struck by all that it symbolized. At Mary's request, the poet's ashes were buried at the English cemetery in Rome beside the body of her and Shelley's beloved young son William.

Shelley Museum, Bournemouth

Byron's Allegra
*Born to Claire Clairmont
and Byron, Allegra was
soon caught in a bitter
tug-of-war between them.
Byron would not allow
Claire to see her and
eventually put her into a
convent. Tragically, when
Allegra was just 5, she
caught typhoid and died
before either Claire or Byron
could reach her.*

iams' safe arrival in Leghorn. There was a terrible thunderstorm which they thought would have delayed the two men's departure for home. But then they waited – and waited – for their return.

Mary later wrote, 'To tell you all the agony we endured during those 12 days would be to make you conceive a universe of pain – each moment intolerable and giving place to one still worse.' Their worst fears were finally confirmed when Shelley's and Williams' bodies were washed up on the shore on 18 June 1822.

LIFE WITHOUT SHELLEY

In the days that followed, Mary was overwhelmed with despair. She longed to die, but the future of her son depended on her. So she unwillingly pulled herself together and made plans to stay in Italy and work, in the hope that she would be helped by an allowance from Shelley's family. But when his father wrote that he would maintain her son, Percy, only if she gave him up, she refused and returned reluctantly to England. Here she met up with Jane Williams again and felt the beginnings of a love which was not to be reciprocated, although the two women were to spend much time together.

Faced with lack of money and dismal lodgings, she struggled to write her next novel *The Last Man*. It was then that she heard of Byron's death and more than ever saw herself as the 'last man', "girded, walled in, vaulted over, by seven-fold barriers of loneliness".

In 1827 Jane Williams went to live with Hogg, with whom she had been having a love affair for some years. Away from Mary she began to gossip about the Shelleys' relationship, trampling on Mary's precious memories. Many of Mary's other old friends were to turn against her in later years. They regarded her as a cold, unemotional, conventional woman who disappointingly rejected the radical beliefs of her husband in favour of society's approval.

Meanwhile little Percy was fast becoming the only male to whom she could give her love. He was never to show any signs of genius, but he was an affectionate, easy-going boy and, eager to give him a good education, she sent him as a day boy to Harrow at the age of 12. Her life was now poverty-stricken and solitary.

LESS TROUBLED DAYS

Mary eventually began to enjoy a middle age in which she travelled to the Continent with Percy and wrote various pieces of non-fiction. And in 1844, when Shelley's father, Sir Timothy, died, leaving his estate and baronetcy to his grandson, her money worries were over. Unfortunately her new status made her vulnerable to blackmail attempts . She fought them but the attacks on her privacy took their toll on her health.

Mary had tired of life by the time she met her son's wife-to-be, Jane St John, in early 1848. Jane was a young widow who quickly became a devoted friend. She contributed much to what happiness Mary enjoyed in the last years of her life. In the winter of 1850, Mary became increasingly paralyzed and, knowing she was dying, passed on to Jane the care of Shelley's papers and reputation. On 1 February 1851, Mary Shelley died.

Fairner: The Funeral of Shelley, Walker Art Gallery, Liverpool

FRANKENSTEIN

The strange, haunting story of Frankenstein and the Monster he created and abandoned came to Mary Shelley in a dream-like vision. For Frankenstein himself, his dream became a nightmare.

However familiar we may be with the story of Frankenstein and his monster – now a part of popular culture – Mary Shelley's *Frankenstein*, published anonymously in 1818, is still an extraordinary tale. It is written with a passionate intensity and extravagance of style that is in keeping with the Gothic romances of the day, but the extremes of feeling expressed by the characters reflect the enormity and horror of Frankenstein's achievement. The novel's real fascination lies in its imaginative power and the gradual awakening of Frankenstein and his creation to the entwined tragedies that are their fate.

GUIDE TO THE PLOT

The story begins almost at the point where it ends. Robert Walton, idealist and Arctic explorer, discovers Victor Frankenstein dazed and near-death on the ice floes of the North Pole. He takes him on board ship, and writes down Frankenstein's story in the form of letters which he sends home to his sister.

Victor begins his tale by describing his idyllic childhood as the eldest son in a wealthy Genevan family. His desire to learn "the secrets of heaven and earth" take him to the 'wrong' books of alchemy and magic. Later, after several years of intense study of 'natural philosophy' at Ingolstadt University, he discovers "the cause of generation and life; nay more, I became myself capable of bestowing animation on lifeless matter."

He intends his creation to be beautiful, but is faced with a creature so hideous he cannot bear to look at him. The Monster follows him to the bedchamber, holding out his hand, but Frankenstein flees in horror, appalled at what he has done. The creature has disappeared by the time Frankenstein returns to his lodgings. An old childhood friend Henry Clerval comes to see him, and (knowing nothing of Victor's dreadful secret) spends the winter nursing Victor through a delirious fever until he is well enough to travel home. Before they leave for Geneva, Victor hears from his cousin Elizabeth that his young brother has been murdered. The boy's nursemaid is hanged for the crime, but Frankenstein knows the killing is the work of the Monster. Beside himself with grief and remorse, Victor seeks refuge and solitude in the mountains.

On the glacier at Chamonix, the Monster compels Frankenstein to listen to his story. He describes his first encounters with people who flee from him in fear and disgust; how he learnt the rudiments of survival; how he observed a family through a crack in their cottage wall and so learnt language as well as a sophisticated grasp of the history of civilization. Longing for companionship, he had made himself known to the family but once again was driven away. He then resolved to find Frankenstein, his creator, and ask him for help and comfort.

"I am malicious because I am miserable", the Monster cries. He appeals to Frankenstein to make him a mate, a female "as deformed and horrible as myself" with whom he promises to leave Europe and live in "the most savage of places", troubling no-one. Frankenstein grudgingly agrees, and sets off on a jour-

> "It was already one in the morning; the rain pattered dismally against the panes, and my candle was nearly burnt out, when, by the glimmer of the half-extinguished light, I saw the dull yellow eye of the creature open; it breathed hard, and a convulsive motion agitated its limbs."
>
> FRANKENSTEIN

Awasowski: Iceberg, Bildergalerie, Feodossija.

Solitary search
(above) Frankenstein's quest for the secrets of life leads him to withdraw from humanity. He seeks refuge and consolation in the "sublime", isolated mountains.

A dangerous journey
(left) Walton, the narrator, is unsure whether to turn back from a voyage of discovery in the Arctic. But his meeting with the dying Frankenstein helps him to decide.

C. E. Kuwasseg: St. Etienne: Bridgeman Art Library

C. D. Friedrich: Wanderer Above the Mists. Kunstalle, Hamburg

Detail from "The Alchemist" by Joseph Wright. Derby Art Gallery

ney to England with Clerval, settling finally in a hut on a remote island in the Orkneys by himself to create a female monster.

When this second of his creations is almost complete, Frankenstein panics and destroys his work, for fear of peopling the world with monstrous offspring. The Monster, waiting outside the hut, swears revenge: "I go; but remember, I shall be with you on your wedding night." Frankenstein must endure the deaths of two more loved ones at the hands of the Monster, before setting out across the arctic wastes to pursue and destroy his creation once and for all. He is led on across oceans and continents by taunting messages: " . . . Follow me; I seek the everlasting ices of the north, where you will feel the misery of cold and frost, to which I am impassive."

The tragedy is concluded in Walton's words, in a final letter to his sister, in which he writes: *"Great God! what a scene has just taken place! I am yet dizzy with the remembrance of it. I hardly*

know whether I shall have the power to detail it; yet the tale which I have recorded would be incomplete without this final and wonderful catastrophe . . ."

VISION OF HORROR

Frankenstein was greeted with shock and amazement when it first appeared. Containing many elements of the fashionable Gothic novel, the story nevertheless stunned contemporary readers. Mary Shelley gave an explanation as to its origin in an introduction to a later edition of the novel. The idea of writing a 'ghost' story came from Byron, the Shelleys' neighbour in Switzerland. Mary took some time to develop a tale "which would speak to the mysterious fears of our nature and awaken thrilling horror – one to make the reader dread to look round, to curdle the blood, and quicken the beatings of the heart".

A discussion about the discoveries of Erasmus Darwin, and about whether it might actually be possible to manufacture a 'creature' triggered a powerful image in her mind: 'When I placed my head on my pillows I did not sleep, nor could I be said to think . . . My imagination unbidden, possessed and guided me . . . I saw – with shut eyes, but acute mental vision – I saw the pale student of unhallowed arts kneeling beside the thing he had put together. I saw the hideous phantasm of a man stretched out, and then, on the working of some powerful engine, show signs of life and stir with an uneasy, half vital motion. Frightful must it be; for supremely frightful would be the effect of any human endeavour to mock the stupendous mechanism of the Creator of the World . . .'

The rest of the story unfolded from this central, awe-inspiring image. Like Walton, the reader awaits the confessions of Frankenstein with excitement and trepidation, for "strange and harrowing must be his story". But Frankenstein is hardly a 'ghost story',

Tranquil lakeside
(above) Frankenstein delights in the refinement and gentle beauty of his lakeside home. But when the Monster appears there, the little town is rocked by horror.

'Unhallowed arts'
(left) Mary Shelley described her 'hero' as a 'student of unhallowed arts'. His eagerness to pioneer great scientific advances which could benefit his fellow humans has terrifying consequences.

13

except in its power to frighten and horrify. It deals with more sophisticated concepts than ghosts and ghouls, and weaves a creation myth so perverse that death and destruction can be the only outcome. Mary Shelley was concerned not just with terror, but with 'the elementary principles of human nature'. She was writing in an age when the first discoveries of modern science were being explored, an era of dawning possibilities. And *Frankenstein* is a haunting psychological study, within a framework we would call 'science fiction' today, of a man whose idealistic desire

A lonely school
(right) In a remote cottage, the Monster finds a family fallen upon hard times. He keeps himself hidden, but eavesdrops, and gains an education in language, culture and family love. When he dares to show himself to them he learns a more painful lesson.

C. D. Friedrich: Abend am Fluss (Detail). Museen der Stadt, Köln

> "Everywhere I see bliss, from which I alone am irrevocably excluded. I was benevolent and good; misery made me a fiend."
>
> THE MONSTER

to unlock the secrets of Nature leads to unforeseen tragedy.

FORBIDDEN KNOWLEDGE

Mary Shelley's book is subtitled 'The Modern Prometheus'. In both Greek and Roman legend Prometheus was a creator, giving fire to mankind, or in some stories creating Man himself from clay. He was cruelly punished by Zeus (the supreme god on Olympus), but by then Prometheus' deed was done – the

world was peopled with unruly humans who could live independently of the gods now they had the gift of fire. Mary Shelley cast Victor Frankenstein in the Promethean role, making him a modern scientist in search of the spark to animate lifeless matter. He is punished as forcefully as Prometheus was, for meddling in the work of the gods.

Frankenstein describes his obsessive search for the secrets of nature, and how his concentrated reading and study take him further and further away from the family and values he professes to love. And still he cannot rest: *"No-one can conceive the variety of feelings which bore me onwards, like a hurricane, in the first enthusiasm of success . . . A new species would bless me as its creator and source; many happy and excellent natures would owe their being to me . . ."*

But Frankenstein's creation does not herald a happy wondrous new species: "His yellow

In the Background

PROMETHEUS

I n Greek and Roman mythology, Prometheus, the immortal giant, was the champion of humankind. He moulded people out of clay, and stole fire for them from the gods' home on Mount Olympus. When Zeus, leader of the gods, looked down on Earth and discovered that Man had received the gift of fire – and hence of independence – he determined to punish Prometheus.

Prometheus was sentenced to be chained to a rock, and to have his liver pecked out by an eagle in a never-ending torture. He was finally freed by Hercules.

For the Romantics, Prometheus was a symbol of artistic achievement, a hero who dared to defy the forces that would prohibit his creative endeavour. To them he was an anti-establishment rebel who was concerned with progress and intellectual enlightenment. He .features in Percy Bysshe Shelley's poem *Prometheus Unbound.*

G. S. Watson: Prometheus Consoled by the Spirits of the Earth (Detail). Fine Art Photographic Library

Innocent victims
(left) The youth, purity and gentleness of the Monster's victims highlight the atrocious nature of their deaths. After his first murder, the Monster exclaims in "exultation and hellish triumph . . . 'I too can create desolation; my enemy is not invulnerable'".

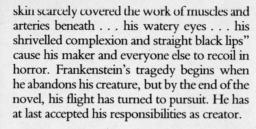

Goya: The Third of May (Detail). Prado, Madrid/Estidio

skin scarcely covered the work of muscles and arteries beneath . . . his watery eyes . . . his shrivelled complexion and straight black lips" cause his maker and everyone else to recoil in horror. Frankenstein's tragedy begins when he abandons his creature, but by the end of the novel, his flight has turned to pursuit. He has at last accepted his responsibilities as creator.

FALLEN ANGEL

The Monster, from his first "convulsive motion", is described as "hideous", "loathsome", "deformed", "an abortion and an anomaly", a being quite impossible to love. Yet he was not born evil, or morally monstrous, and love is all he craves. Because he is physically monstrous, he is perpetually rejected. His sad tale of longing for warmth and human companionship is immensely moving: "am I not alone, miserably alone?". In desperation

he returns to his maker and voices his misery. His request for a mate seems only reasonable: "I was benevolent and good, misery made me a fiend. Make me happy and I shall again be virtuous." But Frankenstein fears that another creature will simply double the evil.

Mary Shelley prefaced the novel with a quote from Milton's *Paradise Lost*:
  Did I request thee, Maker, from my clay
    To mould Me man? Did I solicit thee
      From the darkness to promote me?
The Monster likens himself to Adam from Milton's *Paradise Lost*: "Remember, that I am thy creature, I ought to be thy Adam; but I am rather the fallen angel, whom thou drivest from joy . . ." For because he has been hated and rejected by all, he also likens himself to Satan, the fallen archangel who was expelled from Heaven and became the Devil in *Paradise Lost*.

There are no clear-cut statements about good and evil, as there would have been in a simple Gothic horror story. The Monster appears evil, but he has been given no chance to be otherwise. Indeed, Frankenstein is perhaps the more evil of the two. "You accuse me of murder," cries the Monster "and yet you would with a satisfied conscience, destroy your own creature." Both set out to be good and the ambivalence between concepts of good and evil is part of the bond between them. And when the two finally come together, they merge in a strange and haunting vision of good and evil, creator and creation, ice and fire . . .

"I shall be with you on your wedding night!"
(left) Frankenstein believes that his only hope of redemption lies in marriage to the pure and selfless Elizabeth. He intends to tell her his dreadful secret — but the Monster intervenes . . .

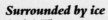

Surrounded by ice
(right) The awesome image of remote ice floes begins and ends the story. Though Walton's ship eventually escapes the groaning pack-ice, Frankenstein's fate is sealed. He cannot return to humanity.

Kersting: Before the Mirror. Kunsthalle zu Kiel

C. D. Friedrich: Arctic Shipwreck (Detail). Kunstalle, Hamburg

CHARACTERS IN FOCUS

Frankenstein and his Monster are locked together in a deadly union. Their story is told – through the medium of Walton's letters home – in their own words, which lends poignancy and conviction to their hopes and fears. The other characters serve mainly to illustrate the central tale, and to show that Frankenstein is rich in family and friends while the Monster has no-one. In *Frankenstein*, Mary Shelley created two characters as large and enduring as the original Promethean myth.

WHO'S WHO

Victor Frankenstein The sensitive, educated, tragic hero whose obsessive research leads to untold grief.

The Monster Frankenstein's creation. He describes himself: "I, the miserable and abandoned, am an abortion, to be spurned at, and kicked and trampled on."

Henry Clerval Victor's closest friend who, as a boy, "loved enterprise, hardship and even danger for its own sake".

Elizabeth "The living spirit of love", she is adopted by Victor's family, growing up as his 'cousin' and bride-to-be.

The De Lacey family Felix, Agatha and their blind father are the gentle cottagers who are tenderly observed by the Monster.

Safie The family's beautiful Arabian visitor whose language lessons are secretly shared by the Monster.

M. Waldman The influential professor who inspires Victor at the beginning of his studies.

William Victor's young brother and the Monster's first victim.

Justine William's faithful, trusted nursemaid who is wrongly accused of his murder.

Victor's father A respected, honourable citizen of Geneva. His benevolence and complete faith in his son sustain Victor through disaster and illness.

Walton The romantic arctic explorer with "a love for the marvellous", whom Victor entrusts with his life story.

Francisco Goya: The Idiot

F. R. Pickersgill: The Artists Son & Nurse. Wolverhampton Art Gallery Bridgeman Art Library

The unhappy Monster (above), built from the dead and decaying, his hate mixed with love, pleads with his maker: ". . . am I not alone, miserably alone? You, my creator abhor me; what hope can I gather from your fellow creatures . . .? The desert mountains and dreary glaciers are my refuge."

Justine the nursemaid is treated as a virtual member of the Frankenstein family. But she is charged with the murder of little William, and hanged for the crime.

Professor Waldman (right) encourages Victor to take up the study of chemistry, advising him to apply himself to every branch of 'natural philosophy'. His first lecture fires Victor "with one thought, one conception, one purpose . . . I will pioneer a new way, explore unknown powers, and unfold to the world the deepest mysteries of creation." Waldman is a good man. Thus Frankenstein alone carries the guilt for the subsequent misuse he makes of scientific knowledge.

Hermann von Lingg by Franz von Lenbach. Bayer. Staatsgemäldesammlungen, München/Artothek

"The saintly soul of Elizabeth (right) shone like a shrine-dedicated lamp in our peaceful home. Her sympathy was ours; her smile, her soft voice, the sweet glance of her celestial eyes, were ever there to bless and animate us." Victor's childhood sweetheart waits with perfect patience while he completes his studies, languishes in his sick bed and in prison, and agonizes over the projected wedding. He thinks he can protect her from the Monster – even, perhaps, on his wedding night . . .

Friedrich Georg Kersting: "Die Kranzwinderin". Nationalgalerie, Staatliche Museen Preussischer Kulturbestz. Berlin (West)

"Henry Clerval . . . a boy of singular talent and fancy" (below) makes a striking contrast to Victor, for he remains optimistic, happy and enthusiastic as Frankenstein declines into illness, hopelessness and despair. Can this "perfectly humane, so thoughtful" friend rescue Victor from the brink of self-destruction?

Portrait of Pierre Narcisse Guerin by Robert Lefèvre. Musée des Beaux-Arts, Orléans/Lauros-Giraudon

(right) Frankenstein is the "modern Prometheus", who dares to hope that he could create "a new species [which] would bless me as its creator and source". Instead he creates a being which seems so monstrous that he abandons it. The narrator Walton admires Frankenstein, because his mind is so cultivated. But his is a brilliant intellect destroyed by the consequences of its own genius.

Gustav Hellquist by Ludwig Thiersch. Bayer. Staatsgemäldesammlungen, München/Artothek

DARK IMAGININGS

Inspired by Romantic ideas and personalities, Mary Shelley's grand, visionary works often echo the torments of her own life. Her expansive imagination captured the spirit of the age.

The woman who wrote *Frankenstein* had a very modest opinion of her own talents. Years after the novel was published, Mary Shelley remarked despairingly in a private letter that 'I should be happy if anything I ever produced may exalt and soften sorrow . . . But how can I aspire to that?'

Along with this humility went a curious reluctance to discuss herself or her own work. Her letters and journals contain only passing references to her writings: 'I am very averse to bringing myself forward in print', she confessed in her introduction to the 1831 edition of *Frankenstein*. This was the only occasion on which she wrote at any length of how she conceived and wrote books.

Frankenstein established Mary Shelley as a successful writer when she was in her early twenties. Her husband's later fame as a poet makes it easy to forget that during his lifetime she was a better known literary figure than he was. But *Frankenstein* triumphed despite a mixed reception from the critics.

The *Quarterly Review* raged against the 'tissue of horrible and disgusting absurdity this work presents', prejudiced by its dedication to Mary's father, the notorious radical, William Godwin. But Sir Walter Scott warmly praised 'the author's original genius and happy power of expression', although he and many others assumed that *Frankenstein* had been written by Percy Shelley. When they discovered the author was the poet's very young wife, they were astounded. Their feeling was expressed by *Blackwood's Magazine:* 'For a man it was excellent, but for a woman it was wonderful.'

The public verdict was clear – *Frankenstein* was a best-seller which kept its popularity year after year. When Mary returned from Italy after Shelley's death, she found that a dramatized version of the novel was being performed at the English Opera House – the contemporary equivalent to a film being made from the original. And in the House of Commons, 'Canning [the foreign secretary] paid a compliment to *Frankenstein* in a manner sufficiently pleasing to me.'

Reticent though she was, Mary Shelley did

A model hero
(right) Lord Byron clearly excited Mary's imagination as a romantic figure, for he appears, thinly disguised, in Lodore, Valperga *and* The Last Man. *It was his idea that the friends visiting him at Villa Diodati should each attempt a ghost story, thus inspiring Mary to write* Frankenstein.

Detail from the portrait by Richard Westall. National Portrait Gallery

Villa Diodati
During the remarkable summer of 1816, Mary and Shelley gravitated to Byron's house on the shores of Lake Geneva (below) near which they were staying. It is hardly surprising that the spectacular lake and mountain scenery of the area had a dramatic effect on the plot and atmosphere of the book Mary wrote there.

state her literary creed: 'a fiction must contain no glaring improbabilities, and yet it must never divest itself of a certain idealism, which forms its chief beauty'. 'A certain idealism' evidently meant a significant depth and perhaps a larger-than-life quality incompatible with pedestrian realism. Certainly Mary Shelley tended to avoid everyday settings and events in her fiction.

A NEED TO SELL

Frankenstein, The Last Man and a handful of short stories, represent Mary Shelley's fantastic and futuristic vein. But she also wrote about the violent and colourful past. Her second published novel was *Valperga* (1823), a tale of medieval Italy 'raked out of fifty old books', according to her husband. Percy Bysshe Shelley thought *Valperga* better than Sir Walter Scott's historical novels, and Godwin hailed it as 'a work of more genius' than *Frankenstein* – although he complained of its inordinate length.

Valperga proved as commercially successful as *Frankenstein*. By the time it was published, Shelley had been drowned and Mary, left to provide for herself and her son Percy Florence, was about to return to England. But she had assigned all the profits from the book to her perpetually penniless father. She now became a professional writer in the full sense, compelled to please the public if she was to survive.

Her third novel, the apocalyptic fantasy *The Last Man* (1826), was as ambitious as *Frankenstein*, but it was received without enthusiasm. Tastes had changed, and this was probably why Mary wrote no more novels in the highly imaginative vein that we value most. *The Last Man* proved to be her last novel (though by no means her last story) of real merit. However, *Lodore* (1835), a society novel, achieved popular success, possibly because it contained so many characters and episodes that, as readers knew very well, were drawn from Mary's own life.

Mansell Collection

Age of discovery
(left) The vogue for scientific discovery lit the 19th-century imagination, as awesome powers suddenly seemed to be within reach.
Out of this atmosphere of excitement – half superstitious – half rational – came Mary Shelley's fantastic notion of a creature assembled in a laboratory and given life by a scientist.

Percy Bysshe
It was thought, when Frankenstein *came out, that Mary's poet husband (left) must have been the author because 'for a woman it was wonderful'. Shelley was immensely proud of his young wife's achievement and encouraged her in its progress, for he – unlike Byron – thought the ideal wife should be her husband's intellectual equal.*

Shelley Musuem, Bournemouth

PUBLIC SCRUTINY

After *The Last Man*, Mary Shelley published only three novels in 25 years. Her imaginative work was out of fashion and, increasingly anxious for social acceptance, she was painfully conscious that everything she wrote was being read with an eye to its bearing on the scandalous lives of the dead poets Shelley and Byron. This scrutiny seems to have had an inhibiting effect that progressively impaired Mary's creativity. She evidently found it less stressful and emotionally demanding to perform other literary labours – to produce a piously admiring edition of Shelley's poems (1839), or to write *The Lives of the Most Eminent Literary and Scientific Men* and *Rambles in Germany and Italy*.

19

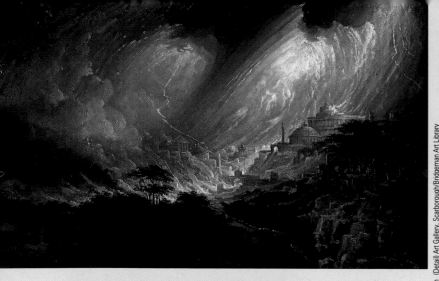

John Martin: Destruction of Sodom & Gomorrah (Detail) Art Gallery, Scarborough/Bridgeman Art Library

Apocalypse
Scenes of ultimate destruction (above) are a hallmark of Mary's greatness. Even before her life was overwhelmed by tragedy, her mind was full of cataclysmic images.

Shades of Byron
In the short story Euphrasia, *a Byronic hero rescues his sister from a Turkish harem (left). But she is shot dead in his arms while his fate is to die in the Greek cause.*

Sublime Nature
Frankenstein himself expresses the Romantic notion of the Sublime quality of magnificent natural scenes such as this alpine landscape (right) – ". . . although they did not remove my grief, they subdued and tranquillised it".

Readers who looked for autobiographical references in Mary Shelley's fiction were rarely disappointed. Characters and incidents from the earlier part of her life appear again and again in her work, either in remembered detail or reworked into might-have-been episodes.

Mathilda, written just before *Valperga* (but not published until 1959), reflected her passionate attachment to her father, fusing incestuous fantasy about the past with the reality of her own immediate grief as a bereaved parent. Much more of Mary's writing drew on her eight years as Shelley's companion and wife. For example, their debt-ridden days in London are described in *Lodore,* and in *The Last Man* the Shelley-figure Adrian perishes by drowning, as did the real Shelley. (Uncannily, the same fate befalls Mathilda's father, in the story written while Shelley was still alive.)

MALE LEADS
The images of Shelley and Byron inspired most of the leading male characters in Mary's best novels and stories. Shelley is clearly the model for the devoted Woodville in *Mathilda* and the unworldly, unattached Adrian in *The Last Man*. But these are idealized versions of the real poet, who was more complex, more

sensual and less dependable than Mary's fictional figures. Both as a novelist and an editor, Mary helped to make Shelley respectable, by turning him into the archetypal 19th-century Romantic poet: 'a beautiful and ineffectual angel' beating his wings in the void.

By contrast, Mary did justice to both the virtues and the faults of the man she nicknamed 'Albé' – Lord Byron. It is 'the dear, capricious, fascinating Albé' – not Mary's husband – who dominates her fiction. He is clearly the model for Castruccio in *Valperga,* Lodore in the novel of that name, and Lord Raymond in *The Last Man*. His impetuous, heaven-challenging figure had a strong appeal for Mary, much to the annoyance of her stepsister Claire Clairmont, whose hatred of Byron, her sometime lover, grew

fiercer with the passing years. On the publication of *Lodore* she wrote angrily to Mary:

'Mrs Hare admired *Lodore* amazingly; so do I, or should I, if it were not for that modification of the beastly character of Lord Byron of which you have composed Lodore. I stick to *Frankenstein,* merely because that vile spirit does not haunt its pages as it does all your other novels, now as Castruccio, now as Raymond, now as Lodore.'

She goes on to lament that 'a person of your genius' should 'think it a task befitting its power to . . . pass off as beautiful what was the merest compound of vanity, folly, and every miserable weakness that ever met together in one human being!' Mary Shelley, more sympathetic to Byron's personality, even awarded the fictional Raymond prizes

Terrible isolation

Mary Shelley's vision of humanity tormented and outcast is expressed in the central characters of Frankenstein *and* The Last Man. *Her images of horror are paralleled in visual art by her contemporary, William Blake, the visionary painter and poet who conveyed with unique power a remorse-stricken Cain fleeing the scene of his brother's murder (right).*

rations, and insisted that the authors must adapt their stories to fit the pictures.

In reality, Mary Shelley probably benefited from the need to make her tales short, and some of them are among her best works. Her brand of fantasy was evidently more acceptable in this form, and she wrote a number of stories on 'science fiction' themes such as seeming-corpses that are brought back to life after a lapse of centuries, and the consequences of two people exchanging bodies.

In *The Mortal Immortal*, the immortal narrator remains ever young while his wife grows old and querulous – exactly the situation in which Mary Shelley found herself, (although Percy Bysshe Shelley enjoyed eternal youth and immortality in a different sense). Mary had something in common with the hero of *The Last Man*, and wrote, as she looked back at the circle of genius she had once known: *'The last man! Yes, I may well describe that solitary being's feelings, feeling myself as the last relic of a beloved race, my companions extinct before me.'*

Gloomy foresight

Preoccupations with death, decay and ghoulishness (right) were not peculiar to Mary – they were a facet of the Gothic. But there was plainly a morbid streak at work in her writing. Did she perhaps feel gloomy intimations of the future? At the age of 44 she revisited the spot where she had written Frankenstein *and, reviewing her life, saw that 'storm and blight and death had . . . destroyed all'.*

that had eluded the flesh-and-blood poet – she made him a man of action, and the victorious leader of the Greek revolt.

SCIENCE FICTION

Short stories provided Mary with an important source of income after Shelley's death. Most of the stories were written for gift books such as *The Keepsake* – lavishly produced annuals that were a popular feature of the early 19th century. Mary Shelley complained that there was not enough space in the annuals to develop an idea properly: 'When I write for them, I am worried to death to make my things shorter and shorter – till I fancy people think ideas can be conveyed by intuition.' Another constraint was that the proprietors of the annuals often bought engravings as illust-

A parable on scientific obsession, and on the brutalizing effect of ill-treatment, *Frankenstein* (1818) was published when Mary Shelley was only 20. An immediate and sustained best-seller, it made her famous. It was followed by *Mathilda*, a long story so revealingly autobiographical that it remained unpublished until 1959. The second of Mary's novels to appear was *Valperga* (1823), a well-researched historical romance that shows a quite different aspect of her talent. After her husband's death in 1822, Mary had to earn a living by writing, and this fact influenced the nature of her output. *The Last Man* (1826) had a subject as apocalyptic as that of *Frankenstein*, but its relative failure turned her towards historical and romantic fiction. Her three later novels are interesting from a personal more than a literary point of view, and her biographical works and travel narratives have inevitably dated. But in magazine stories such as the *The Mortal Immortal* and *The Brother and Sister*, collected in 1976, she shows an impressive and undiminished imaginative power.

MATHILDA

→ 1959 ←

Mathilda, the grief-stricken heroine (below) of this short novel, is Mary Shelley's highly critical self-portrait, written to distract her from brooding on the death of her little son William. After a loveless upbringing by an aunt, Mathilda is reunited with her father, who has travelled abroad since the death of Mathilda's mother. The attachment between them becomes dangerously passionate, and Mathilda's father takes refuge in flight. She pursues him to the sea only to discover his drowned body in a cottage.

Immersed in grief, Mathilda lives in seclusion until the poet Woodville comes into her life. She falls in love with him, but unwisely uses him as an emotional crutch while she luxuriates in her own self-centred sorrow. Then Woodville is called away. Without his selfless care to sustain her, Mathilda's self-indulgence brings its own tragic results. Mathilda was not published until 1959, 140 years after its completion.

Andea del Castagno: Portrait of Pippo Spano. St Apollonia Museum, Florence. Bridgeman Art Library

DOMINVS PHILIPPVS HISPANVS DESCOLARIS · RELATOR VICTORIE THEVCROB

Etty: Study of Mlle Rachel (Detail). City of York Art Gallery/Bridgeman Art Library

VALPERGA

→ 1823 ←

Though the book's anti-hero Castruccio (left) resembles Byron in many respects, he has an insatiable ambition reminiscent of Napoleon Bonaparte who was still alive when Mary Shelley began her novel. This colourful historical romance, set in 14th-century Italy, was inspired by a tombstone Mary had seen. It was in memory of Castruccio, a real prince of Lucca, and bore the words, 'I lived, I sinned, I suffered'. As *Blackwood's Edinburgh Magazine* noted in its review, Mary's intention was 'to depict the slow and gradual formation of a crafty and bloody Italian tyrant of the middle ages, out of an innocent, open-hearted and deeply feeling youth.' Like other tyrants, Castruccio becomes progressively cut off from humanity by his lust for power, which at last brings his career to its fateful climax. Percy Bysshe Shelley declared 'I know of nothing in Walter Scott's novels which at all approaches the beauty and sublimity of this – creation.'

Hadrian's Villa, Tivoli by Piranesi. British Library

John Martin: Sadak in Search of the Waters of Oblivion. Southampton City Art Gallery

THE LAST MAN

✦ 1826 ✦

Destruction and downfall (above and right) are the recurring themes of this immense, visionary achievement. By the year 2073, England has become a republic, but political strife is as intense as ever. The hopes of the royalists rest on Adrian, the frail, unworldly son of the former king. The charismatic, infernally proud Lord Raymond schemes to restore the monarchy, but Adrian's innate republicanism and Raymond's own wayward passions thwart the plan – instead of making a politically advantageous match, Raymond marries for love. However, he eventually becomes Lord Protector of the republic, and impulsively joins the Greeks in their struggle against the Turks. His victorious army reaches the gates of Constantinople only to find that the inhabitants have already been wiped out by a plague sweeping through Asia.

Adrian emerges as an unexpectedly effective leader, but nothing can contain the advance of the disease. Finally he leads an ever-dwindling band of survivors through a lifeless Europe, and sets sail for Greece in the desperate hope of finding sanctuary.

TALES AND STORIES

✦ 1976 ✦

Detail from "The Alchemist" by Joseph Wright. Derby Art Gallery

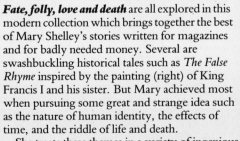

R. Parkes Bonington: Francis I & Marguerite de Navarre. Wallace Collection

Fate, folly, love and death are all explored in this modern collection which brings together the best of Mary Shelley's stories written for magazines and for badly needed money. Several are swashbuckling historical tales such as *The False Rhyme* inspired by the painting (right) of King Francis I and his sister. But Mary achieved most when pursuing some great and strange idea such as the nature of human identity, the effects of time, and the riddle of life and death.

She treats these themes in a variety of ingenious ways. A man in mortal danger changes clothes with his sister – a nun – and is taken over by her destiny. A young man foolishly exchanges bodies with a misshapen dwarf. A 17th-century gentleman is frozen inside a glacier and, when brought back to life a century later, is faced with a world that has changed beyond all recognition. And in *The Mortal Immortal*, the disciple of a famous alchemist (left) swallows one of his master's potions and becomes immune to the ravages of time – with curious consequences.

Gothic Horror

The sensational, the supernatural and the macabre were essential elements of the 'new' kind of novel that thrilled readers of all kinds and classes and made them thirsty for more.

*Y*et tales of terror are her dear delight,
  All in the wintry storm to read at night.

So wrote the poet George Crabbe, describing the fashion for the Gothic novel – a type of story of the macabre and supernatural that had immense popularity during the late 18th and early 19th centuries. The craze for such books was particularly strong in England, but they also flourished on the Continent, especially in Germany, where they were known as *Schauerromane* ('Shudder Novels'). There is much more to Mary Shelley's *Frankenstein* than horror, but all the contemporary reviews treated it as a Gothic romance, and it does indeed use many of the trappings and themes typical of this kind of book – "vaults and charnel-houses" and the "decay and corruption of the human body".

Horror and the supernatural in literature were, even then, part of a long tradition. Some of the standard constituents of the ghost story, for example, go back almost 2000 years, to the Roman writer Pliny the Younger, who told a tale about a large sinister house haunted by a spectre that moaned and rattled its chains at dead of night.

But the Gothic novel broke new ground in its use of situations and props that have since become the stock-in-trade of horror movies: bleak castles, lightning, cobwebbed rooms lit by guttering candles, skeletons dressed in monks' cowls, torture chambers, dungeons, graveyards, gargoyles. The term 'Gothic' originally referred to the medieval settings typical of such stories, but during the late 18th century the meaning changed to suggest a more general notion of remoteness, strangeness and mystery.

IRRATIONAL FEAR

The Gothic novel was one aspect of the very broad movement known as Romanticism, which marked a reaction from the prevailing 'Age of Enlightenment'. Much European thought in the 18th century was characterized by rationalism – asserting the value of reason over imagination. But such a sensible, intellectual stance left unsatisfied a deep-seated human need –

Romantic gloom
(below) When writers in the 18th century invented their tales of horror, they gave the stories such eerie settings as ruined Gothic monasteries and bleak, comfortless castles. The term 'Gothic' originated from the architectural style of the Middle Ages, but came to describe the dark, terrifying tales that achieved such popularity.

The appeal of ghosts

'All were alive to the solemn and terrible graces of the appalling spectre', wrote a commentator, assessing the public's obsession with stories of the supernatural. The Mysteries of Udolpho (below) gave a rational explanation to every outlandish incident, which irked some of Mrs Radcliffe's readers. Homely and shy of publicity, Mrs Radcliffe had no experience of the places she described.

Sex and violence

Matthew Lewis' book The Monk is charged with all the adolescent sexual intensity of the 19-year-old who wrote it. Its heroine Mathilda (above) is captivated by the eloquence of Abbot Ambrosio and enters the abbey disguised as a monk. Her passion for the Abbot arouses his, and devastates these two chaste lives. Because of its explicit violence and sex, there were demands for the book to be banned.

Horror upon horror

Walpole's Castle of Otranto *(spelt wrongly above!) is no literary masterpiece, but its supernatural mystery makes use of elements which were to become the established conventions of the Gothic novel.*

Fuseli's 'Nightmare'

(left) This is one of two versions of a painting by the great Anglo-Swiss artist Henry Fuseli, depicting a woman in the grip of an erotic nightmare. Remarkable for its daring subject matter, it represents not just the outward show of terror but also suggests the dark recesses of the mind.

a need which horror stories could partly satisfy without involving the reader in any personal risk. In 1798, the physician Dr Nathan Drake commented 'Of all the various kinds of superstition which have in any age influenced the human mind, none appear to have operated with so much effect as the Gothic . . . even the most enlightened mind, the mind free from all taint of superstition, involuntarily acknowledges its power.'

The most popular phase of the Gothic novel was from 1765 to 1820. It affected America as well as Europe, and attracted readers of all social classes, from rich intellectuals to poor servants. Some novels were published in sumptuous three-volume editions, others as cheap throw-aways.

THE GRAVESIDE MANNER

Acknowledged forerunners of the Gothic novelists were the 'Graveyard Poets' who wrote reflective, melancholy works dealing largely with human mortality. The best known of these is Thomas Gray, author of *Elegy written in a Country Churchyard* (1751). But the very first Gothic novel is generally held to be *The Castle of Otranto* (1764) by Horace Walpole. Walpole, the 4th Earl of Orford, was a son of Sir Robert Walpole (Britain's first Prime Minister). He was a connoisseur of works of art, as well as a writer, and had an extremely varied career as a man of letters. *The Castle of Otranto* was written at his home, Strawberry Hill at Twic-

kenham (a pioneering work of the Gothic Revival in architecture) and was inspired by a dream: 'I thought myself in an ancient castle . . . and that on the upper bannister of the staircase I saw a gigantic hand in armour.'

Walpole, who wrote the book in under two months, published it anonymously, offering it as a translation 'From the Original Italian of Onuphrio Muralto, Canon of the Church of St Nicholas at Otranto', a 13th-century cleric. Walpole feared ridicule, and to a literary public accustomed to novels of domestic sentiment, his tale must have seemed outlandish. The plot was as labyrinthine as the castle's gloomy passages and vaults. It featured ghosts, giants, and statues that came to life, while its human characters gave unrestrained vent to their emotions. Sensation rather than subtlety was Walpole's strong point – and the public loved it. A second edition was called for within a year, and ten more followed, as well as French and Italian translations.

To modern readers, the book seems convoluted, artificial and not very well written. Certainly it is now hard to credit that after reading it, the poet Thomas Gray (an old schoolfriend of Walpole) was 'afraid to go to bed o' nights'. Walpole himself did not try to follow up *The Castle of Otranto* – and in spite of its success it was some time before imitations appeared. The next Gothic novel with a claim to fame was *Vathek* (1786) by William Beckford.

Sources and Inspiration

Beckford came from a family that had made a vast fortune from sugar plantations in the West Indies (Lord Byron referred to him as 'England's wealthiest son'). He grew into a beautiful young man, but it was rumoured that he was involved in black magic, and one of his female cousins described him as 'a second Lucifer'. In 1784 Beckford was caught in the bedroom of a 13-year-old boy – a nobleman's son for whom he had conceived a passion – and the ensuing scandal caused him to leave England with his wife and daughter.

He returned ten years later, a widower, and lived in eccentric seclusion at Fonthill in Wiltshire. There he built, at frantic speed, an enormous Gothic house – Fonthill Abbey – which was soon regarded as one of the architectural wonders of the age. He collected vast numbers of books and works of art, but in 1822 he was forced by financial pressures to sell the house. Three years later the 280 foot high tower collapsed and crashed through the building.

ORIENTAL ALLURE

Beckford's novel, *Vathek*, was written in French but translated into English. Subtitled 'An Arabian Tale', it is a prime example of the 'Oriental' type of Gothic story, which took the exotic Middle or Far East as its setting. Vathek is a cruel caliph who, in his thirst for power and forbidden knowledge, becomes a servant of Eblis (the Devil). The story is fast-moving and full of dramatic incident, as ghastly crime follows ghastly crime. It sustains the sense of fantasy more effectively than Walpole's book, and ends powerfully with Vathek condemned to eternal torment. Beckford claimed to have written it in three days and two nights while in a kind of trance, inspired partly by the engravings of the 18th-century Italian artist Giambattista Piranesi, who produced a famous series of powerful etchings with

Portrait by Romney. National Trust Photographic Library

William Beckford
(above) He had everything money could buy, plus looks and intelligence, but he dabbled in the occult and disgraced himself with a sexual scandal. Forced to leave England, he travelled in Europe and wrote his oriental fantasy Vathek.

'Imaginary prisons'
The engraving below, made by Giambattista Piranesi as one of a series of nightmarish interiors, was an inspiration to William Beckford and shows a similar concern with the grim and terrifying.

Victoria & Albert Museum

a nightmarish quality, entitled *Imaginary Prisons*.

Whereas both Walpole and Beckford were both very well travelled, the most commercially successful of the Gothic novelists, Mrs Ann Radcliffe, rarely ventured beyond London or Bath, and was such a retiring figure that she was rumoured to have died some time before her actual demise. But she excelled at descriptions of exotic places and the wild forces of nature. Her inspiration came partly from paintings by artists such as the popular 17th-century Neapolitan Salvator Rosa.

Mrs Radcliffe wrote half a dozen Gothic romances, the best known of which is *The Mysteries of Udolpho* (1794). An indication of her popularity is that she was paid a publisher's advance of £500 for this book, then an unprecedented sum. Mrs Radcliffe's tale is set in a gloomy castle in the mountains of Italy, to which the

British Library

beautiful heroine is abducted by her villainous uncle. Various inexplicable horrors beset her, which are all eventually shown to have human origin. Mrs Radcliffe was the chief representative of this 'rational' approach, and in spite of her popularity, some readers felt cheated when apparently supernatural events were ultimately given a prosaic explanation.

EXPLICIT TREATMENT

In *The Mysteries of Udolpho* the heroine's honour as well as her life is threatened, but the sexual element is veiled and timorous compared with its treatment in *The Monk* (1796). Matthew Lewis wrote *The Monk* at the age of 19, when he was attaché at the British Embassy in The Hague. Set in Spain, it is a lurid tale of a once-worthy monk who becomes sexually obsessed, uses supernatural aid to pursue the object of his desires, and finally rapes and murders the unfortunate girl. After being discovered and tortured by the Inquisition, he is hurled to damnation by the Devil, with whom he has attempted to make a pact.

Not surprisingly, this heady mixture of sex and violence caused a sensation, and there were calls for the book to be suppressed. It was excitingly and skilfully written, however, and Lewis was befriended by leading literary figures such as Scott and Byron (Byron

Fonthill Abbey
(above) Beckford's home after he returned from Europe to Wiltshire, was inspired by his intense, flamboyant imagination. It was a folly, a grandiose statement in stone, and it won the same kind of fame as did the Gothic writings of the time. But, having been built at great speed, the central tower of Fonthill collapsed quite suddenly – rather like the vogue for weird and wonderful Gothic.

Mary Evans Picture Library

called him 'Wonder-working Lewis'). To the public at large he became known as 'Monk Lewis'; he never again wrote anything of the quality of his masterpiece.

SHOCKING IMAGES

The fascination with the mysterious, horrific and erotic found in Gothic novels is paralleled in contemporary painting, most notably in the work of Henry Fuseli, for whom Mary Shelley's mother had an obsessive infatuation. Fuseli was Swiss-born (his original name was Johann Heinrich Füssli) and settled permanently in England in 1779. A writer as well as a painter, he was much respected in intellectual circles, and the great poet-painter William Blake described him as:

> *The only man that e'er I knew*
> *Who did not make me almost spew.*

J. Rosierse: Safe from the Storm (Detail) Christie's/Bridgeman Art Library

Pleasure in pain
Agony and torment, inflicted either by human torturers (such as the Spanish Inquisition above left), or by the fires of Hell, often occur in Gothic literature. The voyeuristic sado-masochistic implications are obvious. Readers of such books as The Monk, Vathek and Udolpho were invited to witness the most lurid extremes of human behaviour for their dubious pleasure.

Sympathetic elements
(above) Scenes of fictional horror were almost always accompanied by dramatic weather – illuminated by lightning or lashed by pitiless rain – so as to heighten the atmosphere. Science had been making efforts to analyze lightning's cause and harness its energies. Electricity was held in awe and some people even believed that it could imbue the inanimate with life.

freedom at the price Melmoth asks, and he is condemned to eternal torment.

The plot is involved and potentially repetitive, but the pace never flags and Maturin handles the story with magnificent bravura. Professed admirers of the book have included William Makepeace Thackeray and the painter Dante Gabriel Rossetti. Oscar Wilde called himself 'Sebastian Melmoth' after his release from prison, finding the name of the doomed wanderer appropriate to his plight as a social outcast.

LATER CREATIONS

The Gothic novel did not disappear overnight after *Melmoth the Wanderer*, but it had run its course as the most popular literary form of the day, to be succeeded by the historical novel, of which Sir Walter Scott was the great pioneer. Echoes of the Gothic tradition recur in Victorian literature, however (for example, in Dickens' novels). And the most celebrated of vampire stories, *Dracula* by Bram Stoker, was not published until 1897.

The chilling tale of Dracula's relentless pursuit of his victims has inspired a multitude of horror movies, which tend to highlight the lurid and sensational elements of the tale, rather than its imaginative power. *Frankenstein*, like *Dracula*, has been widely interpreted and promoted on film. Indeed, perhaps the most moving recreation of Mary Shelley's story is the 1931 cinema classic. Boris Karloff's monster, like the original, is not merely bestial – he is a pathetic creature who suffers because of his creator's presumption in trying to usurp the power of God.

Fuseli's most celebrated painting is *The Nightmare*, (1781) an unforgettable image of a woman in the throes of a violently erotic dream. Like Lewis, he shocked his public, but overcame their moral scruples by force of his genius.

SATIRE AND PARODY

By the time Mary Shelley's *Frankenstein* appeared in 1818, the heyday of the Gothic novel had passed. Indeed, in the same year two books appeared ridiculing its conventions – *Northanger Abbey* by Jane Austen and Thomas Love Peacock's *Nightmare Abbey*. Jane Austen is subtle in her satire, but Peacock is gleefully mocking, his characters having names like Diggery Deathshead and Mr Toobad. At the end of the book Scythrop Glowry (a character based on Shelley) thinks of killing himself, but decides instead to open a bottle of Madeira.

The end of the great period of the Gothic novel is marked by the publication of Charles Maturin's *Melmoth the Wanderer* in 1820. It is the only one of Maturin's works which is still remembered, and is perhaps the most powerful of all Gothic novels – one of the few whose reputation has not decreased.

At the outset of the novel, Melmoth is already over 100 years old, having sold his soul to the Devil in return for prolonged life. He can escape from his dreadful pact only by finding someone to take over his part in it, and the plot involves his attempts to persuade a succession of characters to do this. They include a prisoner in the hands of the Inquisition and a man whose children are dying of hunger, but none of the unfortunates will buy

The joy of fear
There is no modern literary equivalent for the massive cult following Gothic books enjoyed. Their appeal overstepped the bounds of class, and the most respectable, refined and genteel of ladies (above) were gripped by the taste for gore, rape and supernatural terror. The absurd extremes to which some novelists went gave rise to Gothic parodies by such wry observers as Jane Austen.

Twentieth-century Gothic
Although Gothic literature burned itself out and largely disappeared during the 19th century, its elements survive today in horror movies and 'pulp novels'. Some motion pictures based on the best of the literature (right) have created legends of their own.

EDGAR ALLAN POE

1809-1849

Morbid, passionate and hypersensitive, Edgar Allan Poe was
brought low by desperate poverty, by the tragic early deaths of all
those he loved, and by the solace he often found in drink and opium.
Yet a wild and vivid imagination transformed the horrors and
obsessions of his life into potent literary material, and he became a
master of the 'Grotesque' and 'Arabesque'. His chilling horror stories
and ingenious tales have inspired countless imitators, and he is now
seen as one of the great American writers.

'A Doomed Genius'

Possessed of an extraordinary literary talent, Poe's life was blighted by poverty, drink and the premature deaths of all those dearest to him. It was only natural that he saw himself as a doomed genius.

A deep and impenetrable shroud of mystery hangs over the life and character of Edgar Allan Poe. The basic facts of his life are known, but the truth about his personality is obscure, for many of those who knew him well died young and the survivors mostly kept their silence. Whatever the truth, his life was as filled with macabre tragedy as his *Tales of Mystery and Imagination*.

The tragedy began almost the moment Poe was born, on 19 January 1809 in Boston, Massachusetts. His mother, the beautiful actress Elizabeth Poe, was barely 21 at the time, but she had already been widowed once and was now beginning to show the signs of the terrible wasting disease tuberculosis. The next year, Edgar's actor father David Poe ran away from his family, to die from tuberculosis 15 months later. So the ailing Elizabeth Poe was left alone with Edgar, his brother Henry and his sister Rosalie, born a few months after David's disappearance.

Henry was left with Elizabeth's parents and, for a while, Mrs Poe was able to support her two children by touring the theatres of the southern states. Her 'childish figure, great wide-open mysterious eyes' and elfin face made her much loved. But her health was declining rapidly, and by late 1811 she was confined to a small, damp room in Richmond, Virginia. Her illness was public knowledge, and it soon became quite the fashion to visit the pale, dying – and destitute – beauty. On 8 December, she died, aged just 24. The image of his mother's young, still, white face was to haunt Edgar for the rest of his life.

FOSTER-PARENTS

One of the visitors to Mrs Poe's death chamber was Mrs Frances Allan, the wife of a prosperous Richmond merchant. When Mrs Poe died, leaving Edgar an orphan, Frances Allan persuaded her husband to take the little boy into their home, while Rosalie was sent to a Mrs Mackenzie. John Allan always resented the presence of this child of 'poor devils of actors' in his house, and the relationship between him and his foster-son was to be bitter and turbulent.

In 1815, John Allan took his family to England, hoping to establish a branch of his firm there. The six year-old Edgar was sent at first to a bleak, disciplinarian school at Irvine in Scotland. But after frantic protests to his beloved 'Ma', he was brought to London to live with the Allans, and went to Manor House School

Boston Harbour
The bustling harbour was the first glimpse many emigrants from Europe had of the New World. Poe's mother arrived there in 1796, and Poe was born in the city in 1809.

in Stoke Newington. His years there gave the young Poe a trace of Englishness which was later to set him apart from his fellow Americans and make his self-consciousness more pointed.

After five years in London, however, John Allan's business was making no progress, and the Allans returned to Richmond, Virginia. Edgar was now growing into a clever, strong-willed but rather sensitive youth and it was not long afterwards that he began to write poetry – many of his poems penned in honour of the Richmond girls attracted to the handsome, dark-eyed boy.

At the age of 14, he fell passionately in love with Mrs Jane Stanard, the mother of one of his school

A tragic mother
Poe was orphaned at the age of three, when his mother (inset, right), the young actress Elizabeth Poe, died of tuberculosis – as his father had. Three weeks later, a fire at the theatre in Richmond where Elizabeth had acted made the bereaved children of actors a focus of public concern. The kind-hearted Mrs Allan persuaded her husband to take Edgar in.

R. Salmon: Boston Harbour from Constitution Wharf (Detail)/Fabri/Bridgeman Art Library

Key Dates

1809 born in Boston

1811 his mother dies; taken in by Allans

1815–20 in Britain with Allans; sent to school at Stoke Newington

1826 goes to University. Runs away and enlists

1829–30 obtains discharge and enters West Point

1831 dismissed from West Point

1835–37 works on *Messenger* at Richmond

1835 marries Virginia

1838 moves to Philadelphia

1843 moves to New York

1845 *The Raven* published

1847 death of Virginia

1849 dies at Baltimore

friends. But his love for Mrs Stanard was doomed, for, apart from the difference in age, Mrs Stanard was, as Poe's mother had been, dying from tuberculosis. It was perhaps the same pale face and red cheeks that he remembered in his mother that drew Poe to Mrs Stanard. She died in 1824, inspiring one of Poe's best poems, *To Helen*.

That same year another pale beauty became the recipient of his ardent protestations – 15 year-old Elmira Royster. And this time Poe's affections were returned. Throughout the summer of 1825, Edgar and Elmira exchanged protestations of undying love and played music together, he playing the flute and she the piano.

By this time, however, the trouble between the wilful young Poe and his narrow-minded foster-father was reaching its peak. Mr Allan was bitterly resentful at Poe's lack of interest in the family business, while Poe seethed at being treated as a charity child. In February 1826, Allan packed Poe off to University in Charlottesville to study law, giving him only a fraction of the money he would need to survive there.

Once in Charlottesville, the 17 year-old Poe gambled to improve his finances – and succeeded only in building up massive debts. Worse still, Elmira's father, disapproving of this young orphan, intercepted Poe's letters to her. Elmira, believing Poe had lost interest, was persuaded to pursue a more 'suitable' match and became engaged to the affluent Mr Shelton. Poe, deep in debt, racked with guilt about his gambling and distraught over Elmira's apparent lack of faith, began to drink for the first time.

Soon, Poe's many creditors were complaining to John Allan, and, in the autumn of 1826, Allan descended in fury on Charlottesville. Poe was withdrawn from the University and dragged back to Richmond, where a series of awful rows ensued. Mrs Allan, now clearly ill from tuberculosis, tried to calm the situation

but to no avail. In March 1827, Poe stormed angrily out of the house, with nothing but the clothes he stood up in, and took a ship to Boston.

Once in Boston, he persuaded a printer to publish a small edition of his early poems called *Tamerlane and other Poems*. But the edition received scant attention, and desperate poverty forced Poe to enlist in the army, under the name of Edgar A. Perry. For 18 months, he was a model soldier, rising quickly to the rank of sergeant-major and writing poetry amid the palms in Fort Moultrie on Sullivan's Island. Yet the prospects for an enlisted man were severely restricted – he could never become a commissioned officer – and Poe was soon writing to John Allan begging for assistance to enter West Point, the officer training academy. Allan did not reply to any of his letters.

By now Mrs Allan was on her deathbed, and Poe

Mr and Mrs Allan
Poe adored his gentle foster mother Frances Allan, but his relationship with John Allan was turbulent and bitter. The proud, wilful young Poe always resented being dependent upon this harsh, authoritarian man, while John Allan resented handing out money to someone he regarded as a wastrel. Like all the women Poe ever loved, Frances died young of tuberculosis, in 1829. John Allan died three years later, cursing Poe.

31

Charleston

(right) When the runaway Poe enlisted in the army under the name Edgar Perry, he was posted to Sullivan's Island in the mouth of Charleston Harbour. This quiet island provided the inspiration for his tale The Gold Bug.

Virginia Clemm Poe

(below) Poe married his beloved 'Sissy' when she was a bright, vivacious young girl of just 13. But over the next ten years, she fell victim to consumption and wasted away, to die in 1847 aged 23. This portrait was drawn moments after she died, when it was realized that no picture of her existed. The original showed her with her eyes closed, but it was later retouched to show the eyes open.

returned to Richmond on 2 March 1829 to find his beloved 'Ma' already buried. In a brief fit of contrition, John Allan offered to help Poe obtain his discharge from the army by paying for a substitute, and to assist his application to West Point. In fact, Allan only gave Poe 12 dollars for the substitute rather than the 75 it would actually cost, and Poe was left owing most of the balance.

In the meantime, Poe was finding a temporary haven in the home of his aunt Maria Clemm, who was living in Baltimore with her two children Henry and Virginia. Also sharing the house were Edgar's crippled grandmother and his alcoholic, consumptive brother. Poe was also achieving his first literary success – a volume of his poems entitled *Al Aaraaf, Tamerlane and Minor Poems* received a good review.

'MUDDY' AND 'SIS'

Poe was enrolled as a cadet officer at West Point in May 1830 and took advantage of his privileges – he published his third book of poems in the same year. But he soon wearied of West Point, and wrote to John Allan begging for permission to resign. By now, Allan was married again, to a woman who convinced him Poe had not 'one good quality', and once more he did not reply. So Poe deliberately neglected his duties, and, in January 1831, was summarily dismissed.

After a cold, miserable month in New York, he returned to Baltimore and a warm welcome from Mrs Clemm and Virginia, now aged nine. Edgar's brother Henry died in August, his grandmother was failing fast and Henry Clemm had become a violent drinker; nevertheless Poe found here the family affection he craved. And soon Mrs Clemm and Virginia, his 'Muddy' and his 'Sis', had become the dearest people in the world to him.

The little household in Milk Street, though, was desperately poor, and the sight of Muddy out begging with her basket for scraps forced Poe to look for ways to earn some money. Seeing a short story competition in a local newspaper, he took himself up to the chilly garret of the Clemm house and began to write the first of the stories for which he is now remembered, keeping himself going through cold and illness with the aid of opium.

In July 1832, he submitted a number of tales, including *Descent into the Maelstrom* and *MS Found in a Bottle* to a competition in the *Baltimore Saturday Visitor*. The judges were overwhelmed by 'the singular force and beauty' of Poe's tales and had no hesitation in awarding him the prize. It was the first real recognition of his extraordinary talent.

The Clemms' circumstances, however, remained so appalling that Poe attempted one last personal appeal to John Allan, now on his deathbed. But as soon as Poe entered the room where Allan lay dying, the bitter old man sat feebly up in bed, waving his cane at Poe and shouting and cursing with terrifying vehemence. Allan died a month later leaving no mention of Poe in his will.

THE YOUNG WIFE

The following year Poe obtained an editorial post on the *Southern Literary Messenger*. But taking the job meant leaving his 'family' and moving to Richmond. Poe was soon lonely and insecure. When he heard that his cousin Neilsen had offered to take Virginia into his home, Poe wrote in anguish to Muddy, begging her incoherently not to agree to this arrangement which would break up his dear home. On the end of the letter he added a postscript for 13 year-old Virginia: 'My love, my own sweetest sissy, my darling little wifey, think well before you break the heart of your cousin Eddy.'

EMACIATED BEAUTIES

All the women Edgar Allan Poe ever loved died young from tuberculosis – his mother, his foster mother, his wife – and he remained morbidly obsessed with pale, consumptive beauties. Women doomed to die young appear again and again in his tales – their bloodless skin, blue-veined foreheads and the "waxen hue" of their pale fingers recalling the fatal symptoms that Poe knew so well.

Maria Clemm
(left) In the home of his 'Muddy' Aunt Maria, Poe found the family he craved. Poe's young wife Virginia was Muddy's daughter. The three of them lived happily together for a decade, helped through many hardships by Muddy's sound practicality.

Mrs Clemm may have suggested the solution – on 22 September 1835, Poe and Virginia were married secretly in Baltimore. Afterwards Muddy, Sis and the delighted Eddy moved to Richmond together and were obviously happy, but Virginia's 'abandoned' affection towards Poe started tongues wagging. In May they arranged a second, public wedding. Virginia's age was evidently an embarrassment, for the affidavit declared she was 'of the full age of 21 years', although she was, in fact, not quite 14.

The Writer's Life

The crisis over Virginia had driven Poe to the bottle; his editor had suspended him from the *Messenger*, warning, 'No man is safe who drinks before breakfast.' But once he was happily settled with the Clemms in Richmond, Poe was reinstated and soon took over editorial control. His stories in the magazine showed his powers were maturing, and he proved to be a brilliant journalist and a devastating critic. In his hands, the *Messenger's* circulation soared, and Poe's name started to become known beyond the South. He was getting bored, however, for 'the drudgery was excessive and the salary contemptible', and started to drink again. When he was dismissed from his post, Poe and his little family set off to conquer the North.

SUCCESS AND DESPAIR

The Poes arrived in New York during a financial crisis, and, after a year of hardship, moved on to Philadelphia in the summer of 1838. The years in Philadelphia proved happy ones, and Poe entered a brief period of success. During his six years in the city, Poe wrote some of his best tales, including *The Fall of the House of Usher*, and consolidated his reputation as a journalist, first as editor of *Gentleman's Magazine*, and then of *Graham's Magazine*. His critical reviews were generally well argued and considered, although they often lapsed into bitter attacks on fellow writers and earned him many enemies.

But his success brought him little money, and, in 1842, there came a devastating blow. One evening in January, Virginia, as pale and large-eyed as Poe's mother, was playing the harp and singing in her sweet, high voice. Suddenly, she caught her breath, coughed, and blood ran down her pure white dress. As Poe

rushed forward to catch her, he realized with anguish that it was the first confirmation that Virginia too was to die from consumption, the terrible disease that had carried off his father, his brother and all the women he had ever loved. Driven 'insane' by despair, Poe took to drinking once more. As her condition grew worse, he drank more and more heavily.

Heavy drinking wrecked his chances of realizing his dream of a high-class, international literary magazine. It

Long Island Farm (above) *Briefly, in the summer of 1844, the Poes found 'a perfect heaven' in the Brennan Farm near New York. Here, in his study with its vast, carved fireplace, Poe completed his famous poem* The Raven.

Sarah Elmira Shelton (above) *In 1849, the widowed Poe persuaded his childhood sweetheart, now a widow, to marry him. But he died just ten days before the set date.*

LITERARY MAGAZINES

In the 1830s and 40s, when Poe earned a meagre living working for magazines such as *Graham's*, across the Atlantic in England literary magazines were in their heyday. Journals such as *Blackwood's* and *The New Monthly* had wide readerships among the rising middle class, and featured work by the greatest writers of the age – Dickens, Bulwer Lytton, Thackeray. Their blend of quality and popular appeal deeply impressed Poe and he asserted that similar magazines 'will (soon) be the *most* influential of all departments of Letters'. In his literary stance, learned tone and taste for the burlesque and horrific, he consciously adopted *Blackwood's* style. America, Poe felt, was sadly lacking in comparable magazines – largely because the 'paltry prices' paid by the American editors meant writers could never create 'elaborate compositions'. He was determined that his journal, to be called *The Stylus*, would never exploit writers as he had been exploited.

The English style
When Poe edited Burton's Gentleman's Magazine *(left), he emulated English editors such as Bulwer Lytton (right).*

Down and out
(above right) The success of The Raven *did nothing to lift the Poes' poverty, and while the critics of New York sang his praises, Poe and his family were freezing in a damp, cold tenement off Broadway.*

also ruined his chance to earn widespread renown by giving a lecture at the White House – he had to be despatched from the city in a drunken stupor the very day the lecture was to be given. Even the ever-understanding Muddy and Sis found it hard to forgive him this time. Yet forgive him they did, and soon the Poes were back in New York.

For two years, life there was as hard as ever. Then, in Spring 1845, Poe's poem *The Raven* was published. The success of *The Raven* was sudden and complete, making Poe a celebrity overnight. Soon fashionable New York literary ladies began to seek him out, and there were rumours of affairs with the established poets Mrs Frances Osgood and Mrs Helen Whitman. Ironically, though, the lack of copyright protection meant that Poe made hardly a cent from his poem, and the Poes were still living in terrible poverty in a New York tenement.

FURTHER GRIEF

Virginia's health was continuing to decline when Poe moved out of the city to a cottage at nearby Fordham. It was plain and simply furnished, but Virginia and Mrs Clemm turned it into a neat home, filled with flowers. Although Poe's acid sketches had alienated the New York *literati*, the literary ladies visited there regularly. Mrs Gove Nichols and Mrs Marie Shew showed particular concern for their poverty, and Mrs Nichols was distressed to see that on her death bed, Virginia had little but straw to keep her warm: 'The coat [Poe's greatcoat from West Point] and the cat were the sufferer's only means of warmth, except as her husband held her hands, and her mother her feet.'

Virginia died on 30 January 1847. Poe was distraught to the point of illness, and his friend Charles Burr claimed: 'Many times after the death of his beloved wife, was he found at the dead hour of a winter-night, sitting beside her tomb almost frozen in the snow, where he had wandered from his bed weeping and wailing.' Mrs Clemm would often sit up all night holding her hand upon his forehead while he lay wracked with grief and fear, or sat at his desk frenziedly writing *Eureka!*.

1848 saw Poe desperately wooing Mrs Helen Whitman and Mrs Annie Richmond, and by December, Helen had agreed to marry him – only to call it off at the last minute. Poe, stung to the quick by the rejection, vowed to quit forever 'the pestilential society of literary women'.

For the first few months of 1849, he worked furiously, writing poems and tales. But his fortunes were still shaky, and, in July, he left Fordham for good, leaving Muddy weeping on the dock at New York. His first destination was his old home town, Richmond, where he was lionized as a celebrity.

THE FATAL MYSTERY

He began to call on his old childhood sweetheart, Elmira Shelton, now a widow, and courted her so ardently that by September they were engaged to be married – on condition that Poe agreed not to drink, a pledge which he kept. Then on 27 September he stopped in Baltimore on his way to give a lecture. What happened there remains a mystery, for he simply disappeared for five days.

On 3 October, an old acquaintance of Poe's, Dr Snodgrass, received a note telling him that there was a gentleman named Poe, 'in great distress' and 'rather the worse for wear, at Ryan's 4th ward polls' where a wild pre-election party was going on.

Dr Snodgrass arrived to find Poe in a terrible state, dressed in borrowed clothes, yet still clutching a fine malacca cane borrowed in Richmond. He was rushed to Washington College Hospital where he fluttered between violent delirium and rambling consciousness for four days. On 7 October 1849, he became quiet, whispered 'Lord help my poor soul,' and died, aged just 40 years.

THE FALL OF THE HOUSE OF USHER
and other stories

These three tales chosen from the collection illustrate the strangely haunting nature of Poe's horror fiction, and his skill and originality as a pioneer of the detective story.

Many 19th century writers were interested in the weird, wonderful and grotesque, but for Poe these aspects of life were an obsession. He concentrated on just a few types of story – horror, adventure, detective and science fiction – but it is this very concentration that gives the stories their haunting quality.

His horror stories dwell exclusively on the macabre and terrifying – disease, death, entombment – and the reader is drawn into a world of unease, anxiety, fear and naked terror. Normality is left far behind, and a mad but logical kind of nightmare prevails. *The Fall of the House of Usher* and *William Wilson* are such stories.

Offset against this type of story are those which reflect Poe's concern with analytical logic and factual or scientific discovery. His detective stories – the first of their kind – are exercises in analytical deduction. In *The Murders in the Rue Morgue* Poe's detective, M. Dupin, solves the crime on the basis of the facts given in newspaper reports.

Poe's science fiction is based on current interests and discoveries, but these often have a strong element of horror. *The Facts in the Case of M. Valdemar*, for example, tells of a man whose imminent death is arrested by

Max Klinger: A Love: Death

The death of Madeline Usher
(above) For many years, Roderick Usher's sister, the lady Madeline, has been dying from a disease which "had long baffled the skill of her physicians". Soon after the narrator's arrival at the House of Usher, she finally succumbs to "the pressure of her malady" and appears to die. Distraught, Roderick prepares to entomb her in the family vaults . . .

mesmerism. The dissolution of his body, and his acute eventual mental torment are documented as a medical history. But this only heightens the sense of horror. As the poet Elizabeth Barrett Browning wrote, 'The certain thing in the tale . . . is the power of the writer, and the faculty he has of making horrible improbabilities seem near and familiar.' This faculty can be seen clearly in the three chosen stories.

The House of Usher
(left) The atmosphere of gloom and decay that cloaks the ancient House of Usher is almost tangible, and when the narrator first looks upon its bleak walls and vacant eye-like windows, he is overcome "with an utter depression of soul". Even the rank grey sedges, the rotting trees and the dark, still tarn (lake) before the house seem to reek of the deadly melancholy that afflicts its owner. Yet despite the decay, the old house seems solid enough – only "the eye of a scrutinising observer" might see the fatal flaw, the barely perceptible fissure that zigzagged down the wall "until it became lost in the sullen waters of the tarn".

Fatal encounter
(right) At the carnival in Rome, William Wilson comes face to face with the namesake and double who has dogged him for years – and determines to confront him in a deadly duel. But the consequences are more terrible than he can imagine.

THE FALL OF THE HOUSE OF USHER

One of Poe's most famous tales, *The Fall of the House of Usher*, is an evocation not only of a macabre imagination, but of a distorted and obsessive frame of mind. The atmosphere of darkness, gloom and foreboding is unrelieved from beginning to end. Poe invites his reader into a landscape that is not real, but perfectly credible – it is the landscape of the believable nightmare. As the tale unfolds, we share the narrator's increasing "sense of insufferable gloom".

The story of *The Fall of the House of Usher* is exceptionally uncomplicated. It hinges on Roderick Usher, the last of his line, who is inexplicably suffering from a dreadful malaise and nervous agitation.

The narrator of the story is an old friend whom Roderick has asked to visit him to help revive his spirits. On arrival at the House of

> "'We have put her living in the tomb! *Said I not that my senses were acute? I* now *tell you that I heard her first feeble movements in the hollow coffin. I heard them… yet I dared not* – I dared not speak!'"
>
> The Fall of the House of Usher

Usher, the narrator surveys the scene "with an utter depression of soul which I can compare to no earthly sensation more properly than to the after-dream of the reveller upon opium". The traveller who comes from the real world – and the reader – immediately becomes aware of the despair pervading this bleak and forbidding place.

The narrator not only learns of Roderick's peculiar frame of mind, but also of his attachment to his sister Madeline, whom he glimpses only once before she appears to die of an incurable illness. Roderick's own condition worsens, and he insists that they place

The imperious schoolboy
(above) As a schoolboy, "the ardour, the enthusiasm, and the imperiousness" of his nature mark William Wilson out from his schoolmates, and give him ascendancy over all of them but one: his namesake.

Madeline's body, in her coffin, in the vaults of the house. This they do, and the visitor stays on for a few more days, until one night a storm brings the two men together. Strange noises, heard above the crashing of the storm, lead to an apparition of the lady Madeline, then to a horrifying dénouement.

The prevailing theme in *The Fall of the House of Usher* is typical of Poe – that of premature burial. Not only is Madeline encased in her coffin while still alive, but Roderick Usher himself is entombed in his own house, oppressed by an atmosphere "which had reeked up from the decayed trees . . . a pestilent and mystic vapour, dull, sluggish, faintly discernible, and leaden-hued". No chink appears in the mental or physical landscape to give a vision of redeeming life or hope.

There is also an element of autobiography in the story. Roderick Usher, whose actions were "alternatively vivacious and sullen", is an embodiment of the manic-depressive at his lowest ebb, and in this reflects Poe's own depressive and delicate sensibilities.

WILLIAM WILSON

William Wilson is an even more patently autobiographical tale. The main character, who tells his own strange story, says of himself, "I am descended of a race whose imaginative and easily excitable temperament has at all

times rendered them remarkable". Poe not only endows his hero with aspects of his own personality, but with his boyhood details.

William Wilson tells of his schooldays, and how his imperiousness soon led to "a supreme and unqualified despotism" over his companions – with one exception. The exception is a boy of his own age, height, looks – and with exactly the same name. He is seen as a threat and a rival: "I secretly felt that I feared him, and could not help thinking the equality which he maintained so easily with myself, a proof of his true superiority." Wilson's antipathy to his double increases the more his rival mimics him.

At Eton, however, Wilson forgets his tormentor and plunges into a life of drunken revelry. But on one such evening he is visited by a stranger who whispers a warning to him, and then vanishes. It is the rival of his schooldays. Later, at Oxford, William Wilson cheats at cards and ruins his opponent. At once a stranger enters " . . . about my own height and closely muffled in a cloak. The darkness, however, was now total; and we

> "From his inscrutable tyranny did I at length flee, panic-stricken, as from a pestilence; and to the very ends of the earth I fled in vain."
>
> William Wilson

could only *feel* that he was standing in our midst". He denounces Wilson, who flees to the Continent to escape the consequences of his humiliation, and the intolerable persecution of his double.

Some years later, at a carnival in Rome, Wilson is brought face to face with his double. Maddened by his persistence, Wilson challenges him once and for all – with disastrous consequences for himself and his oppressor.

The story is not in the habitual Poe vein of the macabre and grotesque, but it has a typical other-wordly and horrific flavour. It gradually becomes clear that the second William Wilson, depicted in more ambiguous terms than the first, acts as the other's conscience. But the point of the story is not simply a moral one. It is also a study of paranoia, the tormenting power of the imagination and the individual's fear of self-encounter.

In *William Wilson*, the reader is left to solve the mystery of the twin characters and work out its implications. But in Poe's detective stories, a dazzling analytical mind – that of M. Dupin – solves the mystery for the reader.

FANTASTIC VOYAGES

Poe shared contemporary enthusiasm for the voyages of discovery that took place in the 19th century. Many explorers wrote accounts of their travels to the Far East, Africa and the North and South Poles, and Poe often reviewed them. His writing reflects the degree of detail he amassed to give credibility to his own fictional seafaring tales – such as *The Narrative of Arthur Gordon Pym*. And in *The Murders in the Rue Morgue*, the plot hinges on the fact that one character has recently visited the Far East.

F. Cayley Robinson: The Call of the Sea

Sir William McEwen Younger Bt./Bridgeman Art Library

E. von Guerard: Milford Sound/Phillips Fine Art/Bridgeman Art Library

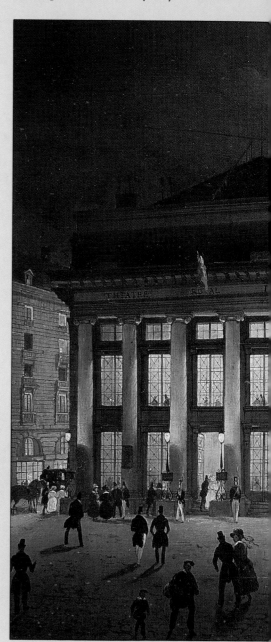

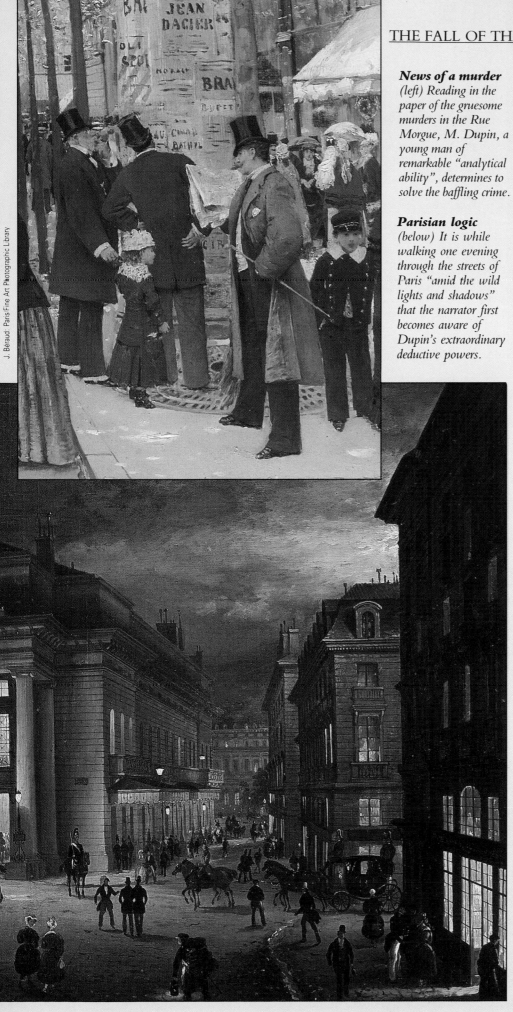

News of a murder
(left) Reading in the paper of the gruesome murders in the Rue Morgue, M. Dupin, a young man of remarkable "analytical ability", determines to solve the baffling crime.

Parisian logic
(below) It is while walking one evening through the streets of Paris "amid the wild lights and shadows" that the narrator first becomes aware of Dupin's extraordinary deductive powers.

THE MURDERS IN THE RUE MORGUE

This, a prime example of Poe's few detective stories, shows the author at his ingenious best. His detective Dupin has qualities of fervour and boundless imagination, but it is his great analytical ability that is brought to the fore.

The story of *The Murders in the Rue Morgue* is, according to the narrator, intended as a means of describing analytical intelligence. He tells of a previous stay in Paris, when he had met a gentleman "of an excellent – indeed of an illustrious family" who had been reduced to extreme poverty. The narrator takes the gentleman, M. Dupin, to live with him in the "time-eaten and grotesque mansion" he is renting. Here he readily adapts to the peculiar nocturnal lifestyle of his guest.

The narrator becomes increasingly impressed by Dupin's unusual powers of deduction and by his claims to be able to read men's hearts – claims which he is able to support "by direct and very startling proofs". Dupin becomes interested in a murder case reported in the newspaper. The crime is reported with objective and horrifically clinical detail. Scorning the ability of the Parisian police, whom he calls "cunning, but no more", Dupin is fascinated by the crime and with his friend inspects the scene in the Rue Morgue.

> *"'. . . a search was made in the chimney, and (horrible to relate!) the corpse of the daughter, head downward, was dragged therefrom . . .'"*
>
> The Murders in the Rue Morgue

What appears to be a bizarre act of savagery is gradually unravelled, to the narrator's amazement, in a process that involves minute examination of the evidence and an unrelenting process of methodical deduction. In response to Dupin's hints, the narrator exclaims, " 'A madman . . . has done this deed – some raving maniac escaped from a neighbouring *Maison de Santé*.' " But the solution is far more unusual than the narrator can imagine, and he finally witnesses Dupin put his conclusions to the test and prove his macabre theory.

The Murders in the Rue Morgue is essentially a tale about the deductive powers of the human mind. But it also questions how people interpret reality. The difference between Dupin and the police is that he analyzes the facts before him more profoundly and acutely, and hence more accurately, than they do. Similarly, the witnesses' accounts of the murders – all telling a different story – reflect the power that the mind has to create its own version of reality.

CHARACTERS IN FOCUS

Although Poe wrote stories to express a theme or unravel a mystery, his characters are seldom mere stereotypes. He pays great attention to physical detail and to foibles and idiosyncrasies, so that even lesser characters have a strong presence. Poe's characters are inseparable from their environment. Thus the imposing House of Usher and the dark Paris streets give weight to the macabre personalities.

WHO'S WHO

The Fall of the House of Usher

Roderick Usher The strange inhabitant of the house. Highly strung and hypersensitive, he is given to morbid fantasy.

The narrator An old friend of Roderick's, whose visit to the House of Usher is more awful than he could ever have imagined.

Madeline Usher Roderick's sister, who succumbs to an incurable disease. Wan and wasted, she is a spectre-like presence.

William Wilson

William Wilson, the narrator A wild and degenerate character, he has the power to manipulate and dominate others, but, ironically, is the 'victim' of the story.

The 'double' Identical to the first William Wilson from boyhood, the 'double' is initially whimsical and cheeky in his rivalry with Wilson. Later he becomes an increasingly haunting figure.

The Murders in the Rue Morgue

Monsieur C. Auguste Dupin A highly intelligent gentleman of good family whose fortune has disappeared. Quiet and observant, he possesses an acutely analytical mind.

The narrator An independent intellectual, who is intrigued by Dupin's personality and story. The two men spend all their time together, reading, talking and walking the streets of Paris.

A sailor A gruff, burly man, recently returned from a voyage to the Indian Archipelago.

The witnesses A random group of ordinary citizens, including a laundress, a gendarme, a tobacconist, a restaurateur and a clerk.

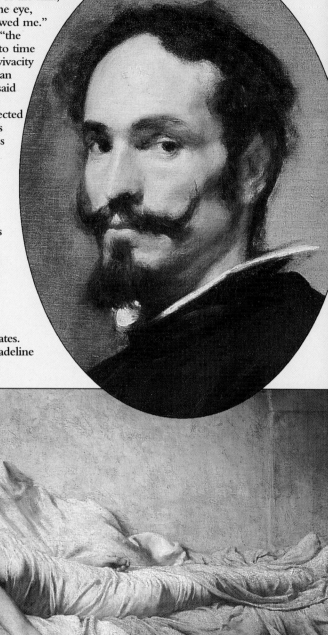

In an atmosphere of "stern, deep and irredeemable gloom", Roderick Usher (right) presents an alarming appearance to the friend (the story's narrator) who visits him. "The now ghastly pallor of the skin, and the now miraculous lustre of the eye, above all things startled and even awed me." He has the inconsistent manner of "the irreclaimable eater of opium", lost to time and place. His mood swings from vivacity to sullenness, and he is gripped by an undefined terror. " 'I shall perish,' said he, 'I *must* perish in this deplorable folly.' " Usher's friend becomes affected by both his spiritual malaise and his fear, and becomes a helpless witness to the man's terrible fate.

THE FALL OF THE HOUSE OF USHER

The lady Madeline (below), Usher's "tenderly beloved sister – his sole companion for long years" is fatally ill of a mysterious wasting disease. Her illness is like a living death, pervading the atmosphere and occupants of the House of Usher. As she weakens, her brother's own depressed and fevered state deteriorates. The narrator has one glimpse of Madeline alive, but it is not to be his last . . .

Fine Art Photographic Library

WILLIAM WILSON

Dominating, wilful and "addicted to the wildest caprices", William Wilson (above) leads a life of vicious self-indulgence. An avid gambler, he systematically cheats "as a means of increasing my already enormous income". Nevertheless, his dissolute companions persist in thinking him "the gay, the frank, the generous William Wilson" – until one night he is caught in the act of fleecing a fellow-student. He is exposed by the one figure able to thwart him – that of his double. Wilson flees, but finds no safe quarter in any of the splendid capitals of the world – "My evil destiny pursued me as if in exultation, and proved, indeed, that the exercise of its mysterious dominion had only just begun." Finally, in Rome, Wilson is about to plunge into an illicit intrigue when he feels "a light hand placed on my shoulder, and that ever-remembered, low, damnable *whisper* . . ."

Walker Art Gallery

Fine Art Photographic Library

The witnesses (below) are ordinary Parisians, living in the Rue Morgue or acquainted with the victims. The newspaper announces that " 'Many individuals have been examined in relation to this most extraordinary and frightful affair' ", and details their evidence. But Dupin calls the police investigations a mere " 'shell of an examination.' " He maintains that to arrive at the truth 'it should not be so much asked "what has occurred," as "what has occurred that has never occurred before." ' He pursues this approach with devastating effect, making the efforts of the police seem woefully crude and uninspired by comparison.

THE MURDERS IN THE RUE MORGUE

Poor but well-educated, Monsieur C. Auguste Dupin (left) impresses the narrator with "the wild fervour, and the vivid freshness of his imagination", and by his extraordinary powers of analysis. The two become friends, habitually taking night walks together, in the course of which Dupin proves his deductive ability by reading his friend's thoughts. For him "most men . . . wore windows in their bosoms". His excitement at proving a theory contrasts with the cool logic of his method.

Fine Art Photographic Library

The sailor (above) is crucial to the solution of the Rue Morgue murders. He is "a tall, stout, and muscular-looking person, with a certain dare-devil expression of countenance . . ." Located by Dupin, he comes to be questioned by him and is immediately on the defensive. He then becomes terrified as he realizes his possible connection with the murders – ". . . the next moment he fell back into his seat, trembling violently, and with the countenance of death itself." But, reassured by Dupin, he says, "I *will* tell you all I know about this affair . . . I *am* innocent, and I will make a clean breast if I die for it."

C. Hunt: A Coffee Stall/Museum of London

MYSTERY AND IMAGINATION

In Poe's tales and poems, images of death, violence and mystery combine. Together they express the bizarre but compelling nightmare vision of his morbid imagination.

Although Poe lived in virtual penury most of his life, his fame and influence as a short-story writer have been widespread, long-lasting and profound. The great French poet, Charles Baudelaire, who translated some of his tales, wrote that if Poe had not existed, he would have had to invent him. And his contemporary Mallarmé said that he learned English simply to read Poe.

GOTHIC HORROR

Poe wrote in the Gothic tradition – that is, his subject matter deals with the macabre and supernatural and his style is characteristically heightened and melodramatic. The themes and settings of his poems often coincide with those of his stories, but it was poetry that was his first and abiding love – 'With me, poetry has not been a purpose but a passion.'

In his poetry, Poe aimed to inspire emotion by the musical effect of words. He would have been pleased by one critic's remark on *Ulalume*, that there was no need to understand English to appreciate the poem, provided it was intoned correctly.

Poe was writing poetry in earnest at the age of 14, and was already displaying traits of morbidity, and of the attraction of death. An early example is the verse he wrote on the death of Jane Stanard, the mother of one of his schoolmates, for whom he harboured a chillingly prophetic infatuation:

> *I could not love except where Death,*
> *Was mingling his with Beauty's breath –*
> *Or Hymen, Time and Destiny*
> *Were stalking between her and me.*

This theme was to recur again and again in Poe's stories as well as his poetry. For him, 'The death of a beautiful woman is unquestionably, the most poetical topic in the world.'

Bettmann Archive Inc/BBC Hulton Picture Library

A gentleman writer
(above) Poe strove for the image of a man of letters. One editor, impressed by his quiet confidence, said, 'Gentleman was written all over him.'

Poe Foundation, Inc. Richmond, Virginia

Fordham retreat
(left) This idyllic cottage was the scene of Virginia Poe's last illness; and here a grief-stricken Poe spent nights composing his prose-poem Eureka.

Harry Clarke: Premature Burial/Weidenfeld Archives

English inspiration
(left) The work of the Romantic poet Samuel Taylor Coleridge inspired Poe's own theories on poetry. Like Coleridge, Poe was fascinated by the world of the unknown and believed that poetry was a way of reaching it. Both poets also used opium regularly.

Premature burial
(left) One of Poe's obsessions was the idea of being buried alive. This fear of being confined, while remaining fully and painfully conscious, occurs in several of his stories, one of which is actually called The Premature Burial. *This illustration for the story conveys the starkness and vividness of Poe's terror.*

The intensity of Poe's vision derived largely from his sense of peculiarity and of separateness from others. This is the subject of another poem, *Alone*:

   From childhood's hour I have not been
    As others were – I have not seen
    As others saw – I could not bring
   My passions from a common spring . . .

This intensity and singularity reach their most haunting – and certainly their most famous – expression in his poem *The Raven*. Despite being much parodied, *The Raven* has at its centre a sense of pain and despair none the less real for being expressed in a theatrical manner:

   And his eyes have all the seeming
    of a demon's that is dreaming,
   And the lamp-light o'er him streaming
    throws his shadow on the floor;
   And my soul from out that shadow
    that lies floating on the floor
    Shall be lifted – nevermore!

The Raven was immediately popular on both sides of the Atlantic. From England, the poet Elizabeth Barrett wrote: 'Your "Raven" has produced a sensation, a "fit o' horror", here in England.' And in his native America, Poe was often called upon to recite it at social gatherings. At occasions when he did so,

Early successes
(left) Poe's stories were initially published in magazines and newspapers. He won a prize of $100 from The Dollar Newspaper *for* The Gold-Bug, *but received his first real literary acclaim for his poem,* The Raven, *which appeared in the* New York Mirror. *For a few weeks he was taken up by the New York literary world, and gave talks and readings to spell-bound audiences.*

43

Deathly beauty
(right) Poe's heroines reflect the nature and preoccupations of his stories. All, from Madeline Usher to Eleonora, are characterized by an unearthly loveliness, a "gorgeous, yet fantastic beauty". But their fascination, for Poe and for us, is that their beauty is linked with the most remorseless and sinister aspects of death.

'. . . he forgot time, spectators, his personal identity, as the wild hopes and repressed longings of his heart found vent in the impassioned words of the poem . . . the auditors would be afraid to draw breath lest the enchanted spell be broken.'

The impetus and obsessive concerns of Poe's stories arose from his precarious mental state, and the strange facts of his life. His heroes are, like him, of a nervous, excitable and imaginative disposition. They frequently show traces of madness – which Poe believed to be a sign of higher intelligence. The narrator in *Eleonora* voices Poe's argument:

Men have called me mad; but the question is not yet settled, whether madness is or is not the loftiest intelligence – whether much that is glorious – whether all that is profound – does not spring from disease of thought – from moods of mind exalted at the expense of the general intellect.

Poe's own extraordinary "moods of mind" led him to focus consistently on the abnormal and terrible in human experience, and present them in a unique and direct way. His control and his author's voice of reason draws the reader into an horrific world from which there is no escape, but which evokes the fascination as well as the panic that is to be found in abnormality.

THE NEARNESS OF DEATH

Because of his wife's illness, Poe had first-hand knowledge of slow, traumatic and bloody death, and this confirmed his own innate morbidity. For him, death was violent, arbitrary and inexorable. The story of *The Masque of the Red Death* is, as it were, suffused in blood:

The 'Red Death' had long devastated the country. No pestilence had ever been so fatal or so hideous. Blood was its Avatar and its seal – the redness and the horror of blood.

To escape it, Prince Prospero shuts himself and his courtiers up in a heavily fortified abbey and entertains them with a masked ball. But despite the revelry, the hourly chimes of the clock cause the revellers to pause:

. . . and, while the chimes of the clock yet rang it was observed that the giddiest grew pale, and the more aged and sedate passed their hands over their brows as if in confused reverie or meditation.

The sense of impending doom is treated with a poetic restraint which makes it all the more awesome and is continued right up to the fateful climax.

Poe's heroines such as Madeline Usher and Eleonora are all mortally sick, like his wife. Eleonora for example,

. . . had seen that the finger of Death was upon her bosom . . . like the ephemeron, she had been made perfect in loveliness only to die.

His heroines' beauty and their ability to command love and reverence are closely bound up with the very fact that they are on the brink of death.

In *Eleonora*, the hero goes so far as to swear always to be faithful to her memory, and "never bind myself to any daughter of Earth. . ." Here we have a glimpse of Poe himself, who in a sense, never forsook the memory of his wife, Virginia. After she died, he became infatuated with a series of 'ideal' women, but none of these passions lasted.

The one constant female figure in his life,

Rebellious hero
(left) For Poe, the ostracized poet Byron epitomized the acute isolation which gives his own writing its peculiar force.

Natural forces
Poe's seafaring tales such as A Descent into the Maelstrom convey the power of Nature against which human life struggles for survival.

Maria Clemm, was Poe's main support and comfort during the painful time when he was writing immediately after his wife's death. She recorded his feverish method of working: 'he never liked to be alone, and I used to sit up with him, often until four o'clock in the morning, he at his desk, writing, and I dozing in my chair. When he was composing 'Eureka' we used to walk up and down the garden . . . his arm around me, mine around him, until I was so tired I could not walk. He would stop every few minutes and explain his ideas to me, and ask if I understood him.'

HAUNTING THEMES

Even when dealing with tales of adventure, or those based on real or supposed fact, Poe's preoccupations remain central to the story. His fear of confinement haunts his seafaring tales, where the expanse of sky and water seems to intensify the smallness and frailty of the craft and of all human life. *A Descent into the Maelstrom* describes in detail a boat and one of its crew of two being swallowed up by a gigantic whirlpool. In *The Narrative of Arthur Gordon Pym*, the hero is

Images of death and torment
Poe explored the dark extremities of the mind, and gave such lucid accounts of what is nightmarish and horrific in human experience, that his images live on and develop in the reader's imagination. Even a literal rendering of the figure of death (left), from The Masque of the Red Death, *has a terrifying power; while the crouching, leering figure (above) suggests the evil spirit of perverseness which Poe saw as a cause of arbitrary acts of violence and destruction.*

a stowaway, and is hidden first of all in "an ironbound box . . . nearly four feet high, and full six feet long, but very narrow, inside the hold." Like Madeline Usher, he finds himself entombed while still alive.

Human perversity is yet another habitual preoccupation with Poe and is frequently linked with the idea of murder. In *The Black Cat*, Poe describes how a normal, humane man inexplicably changes and turns on those he loves. He begins by torturing and then killing his beloved cat – an act from which an obsession develops.

And then came, as if to my final and irrevocable overthrow, the spirit of PERVERSENESS. Of this spirit philosophy takes no account. Yet I am not more sure that my soul lives, than I am that perverseness is one of the primitive impulses of the human heart . . . Who has not, a hundred times, found himself committing a vile or a silly action, for no other reason than because he knows he should not?

This theory underlies the whole of Poe's work and has a powerful psychological conviction. It occurs again in *The Tell-Tale Heart*, where a man is murdered for no motive of passion, revenge or greed, but simply because "He had the eye of a vulture – a pale blue eye, with a film over it." This "unfathomable longing of the soul to vex itself – to offer violence to its own nature . . ." was a hallmark of Poe's own life.

Like his hero, the English Romantic poet Samuel Taylor Coleridge, Poe believed in another, invisible world beyond the world of everyday appearance. His own 'other world' is a haunted, demon-ridden one, but he takes care to present it in a detailed and matter-of-fact way. It is Poe's great achievement that he was able to give shape and logic to his tormented vision. D. H. Lawrence was to say in later years that 'he sounded the horror and the warning of his own doom'. In so doing he captured a dark, but very real aspect of human experience.

45

Master of the macabre, Edgar Allan Poe wove tales of grim tragedy and mystery. He wrote short stories because he could sell them to magazines, but he was a storyteller of hypnotic power. *The Pit and the Pendulum, The Black Cat,* and *The Masque of the Red Death* are classic tales of horror and suspense, while *Arthur Gordon Pym* represents his only attempt at a long narrative. It made him little money, and he subsequently returned to shorter, terser stories. *The Gold-Bug,* a forerunner of a whole genre of cryptic tales, was the first work to make his name. But it was his haunting, nightmarish poem *The Raven* which made him internationally famous.

THE RAVEN

✦ 1845 ✦

The "grim and ancient raven" is the sinister night visitor in Poe's haunting poem. Published in 1845, it made him a celebrity overnight; as he said, 'the bird beat the bug (The Gold-Bug) all hollow'. Rich in atmosphere and symbol, the poem tells of a man who, mourning his lost love Lenore late into the night, is visited by the raven which sits above his door speaking but one word, "Nevermore". As he questions the ghastly bird further, its singular response begins to seem like a chilling prophecy of doom. The poem ends with the man despairing, "And my soul from out that shadow . . . shall be lifted – nevermore!"

O. Redon: The Raven

Harry Clarke: The Pit and the Pendulum/Weidenfeld Archives

Melee on Board the Chesapeake/Bridgeman Art Library

THE NARRATIVE OF ARTHUR GORDON PYM

✦ 1838 ✦

The terrible mutiny aboard the brig Grampus provides a gruesome foretaste of the horrific events to come in Poe's longest tale. The *Narrative* tells of a young man named Arthur Gordon Pym, who is smuggled aboard the *Grampus* in a box, and so begins an extraordinary voyage of adventure at sea. Profoundly influenced by Coleridge's *Rime of the Ancient Mariner,* the narrative describes a living hell as Pym encounters murder, cannibalism, treachery and many other horrors as he journeys South to the Antarctic. Poe researched his subject well, and his tale is remarkable for its detailed and accurate descriptions of life on board ship, while many sections are clearly inspired by accounts of real voyages by the explorer J. N. Reynolds.

THE PIT AND THE PENDULUM

✦ 1843 ✦

The relentless sweep of the pendulum blade as it gradually descends towards him is just one of the horrors that afflict the prisoner in Poe's classic nightmare tale. Incarcerated in utter darkness by the Spanish Inquisition, the prisoner slowly becomes aware of the means his tormentors have devised to ensure his death is long and painful. Poe paints with vivid intensity and gruesome detail the swings between blank terror, despair and awful calm that wrack the prisoner's mind as he survives one torture only to be confronted with one even more terrible. The control of pace is masterly, and Poe screws up the tension to almost unbearable pitch, only to relax it, then apply it again – keeping the reader on the very brink as the prisoner faces the gaping pit, the swarming rats, the scything pendulum, and the redhot walls coming ever closer . . .

Wright of Derby: The Earthstopper/Derby Museum and Art Gallery

THE GOLD-BUG

◆ 1843 ◆

A night-time search for buried treasure forms the climax to Poe's first major success, *The Gold-Bug*. The bug of the title is a mysterious and sinister golden scarab beetle found by an entomologist who, after the discovery, becomes strangely disturbed. At first it seems a classic horror story, but it is in fact a brilliantly contrived mystery tale, which gives full rein to Poe's passion for ciphers and cryptograms. The infallible deductive powers of the hero William Legrand and other Poe figures were to inspire Arthur Conan Doyle's Sherlock Holmes.

Aubrey Beardsley: The Black Cat/Weidenfeld Archives

THE BLACK CAT

◆ 1843 ◆

The black cat is both the unfortunate victim and the one-eyed avenger in Poe's disturbing exposition of the "spirit of perverseness". *The Black Cat* explores a theme which fascinated Poe – a theme he may have seen reflected in himself: that strange element in people which instils in them the urge to destruction and self-destruction. The macabre tale tells of a gentle man who loves animals and marries a wife who fills his home with "bird, gold fish, a fine dog, rabbits, a small monkey, and *a cat*". The cat seems his favourite pet until drink radically alters the man's even temperament. Then, in a spirit of perverseness, he mutilates the cat and kills it. Overcome with guilt, he takes a similar cat into his house – but comes to loathe this too. The story goes on to reveal, with appalling clarity, how the man deals with both the cat and his wife, before the final ghastly twist.

THE MASQUE
OF THE RED DEATH

◆ 1842 ◆

At the masked ball of Prince Prospero, 1000 knights and ladies indulge in a merry and magnificent revel, while outside death stalks the land in the shape of the terrible pestilence, "Red Death". "Blood was its Avatar and its seal – the redness and horror of blood." But isolated inside their castle, Prince Prospero and his court are safe. Only the steady pulse of the vast ebony clock and its discordant chime hint at the impending doom. Yet as the clock strikes midnight, a mysterious masked figure appears in the midst of the revellers, "shrouded . . . in the habiliments of the grave" and "dabbled in blood" – the very image of the Red Death. The tale is melodramatic in the extreme, but the powerful images of blood and the Red Death make this one of Poe's most memorable tales. The relentless progress of the disease finds tragic echoes in the circumstances of Poe's own life – he wrote this tale shortly after he discovered that his beloved wife Virginia was doomed to die from tuberculosis, the malady that destroyed so many of those closest to him.

F. Guardi: Venetian Gala Concert, Alte Pinakothek, Munich/Artothek

Into The Unknown

Poe's weird and wonderful tales reflect an age thrilled by the awesome creations of the Industrial Revolution and inspired by the bold quest of explorers and scientists to unlock the secrets of Nature.

One Spring morning in 1844, New Yorkers were thrilled to see the following late news item in the *Sun* newspaper: 'Astounding intelligence by private express from Charleston via Norfolk! — The Atlantic ocean crossed in three days!! — Arrival at Sullivan's Island of a steering balloon invented by Mr Monck Mason!!' The news spread like wildfire, and before long the whole square surrounding the *Sun* building was besieged by excited people awaiting further news of this fantastic balloon voyage. Within a few days, however, the truth was out; it was all an outrageous joke, a hoax story dreamed up by Edgar Allan Poe, who found the whole venture 'excessively amusing'.

That the public could be taken in so readily by such outlandish stories is symptomatic of a remarkable period in history. In the 1830s and 40s, newspapers reported new sensations with almost monotonous regularity – dramatic balloon ascents, brave voyages of exploration, miraculous tales of corpses galvanized into life, strange secrets revealed in hypnotic trances, and many other amazing events. Some of these stories simply reflected the contemporary fascination for the weird and wonderful, but there were awesome developments in science and technology which were revolutionizing the way in which people lived.

MIRACLES OF ENGINEERING

Remarkable new inventions and engineering feats seemed to appear each year. In 1838 alone, the year of Poe's first stay in New York, New Yorkers could have witnessed the *Sirius*, the first steamship to cross the Atlantic, puffing into New York harbour, followed later the same day by Brunel's wonderful *Great Western* which had set out three days after *Sirius*.

They could have read in the papers, too, of the completion of the London–Birmingham railway, described by the engineer Peter Lecount as 'unquestionably the greatest public work of ancient or modern times'; of the first electric telegraph, installed on the Great Western Railway; of the launch in England of the first screw-driven ship; of suspension bridges spanning broad rivers; and much besides. That same year, in Paris, Louis Daguerre was perfecting the first practical photographic technique, the daguerreotype, which the American inventor Samuel Morse reported in a letter to the New York *Observer* on 19 April 1839.

Poe was one of the first Americans to have his daguerreotype picture taken. And in *The Thousand-and-*

Ascent into the skies
For a century after the first hot-air balloon ascent (right), contrived by the French Montgolfier brothers, people were excited by the potential of such flights. In his hoax of 1844, Poe poked fun at their enthusiasm.

The coming of the railways *(below) Behind the restraint shown by the crowds attending railway openings in the 1830s and '40s lay a sense of awe at the scale and power of those 'fiery leviathans'.*

Mary Evans Picture Library

Giraudon

Joseph Nicephore Niépce: Still Life on Glass

The world's oldest photograph?
(above) Of all the inventions in Poe's lifetime, none seemed as magical as photography. Niépce took this picture in 1827; his partner Daguerre developed the first practical photographic process.

Audubon's birds
(right) The contemporary fascination with Nature attracted many artists to natural history painting. The highly detailed bird paintings in Birds of America (1827-38) are among the most beautiful.

J. J. Audubon: Ivory-billed Woodpecker, Victoria and Albert Museum/Bridgeman Art Library

second Tale of Scheherezade he reveals his fascination for the inventions of his age, describing them in mythic terms. The *Great Western* steamship is portrayed as a great black monster, emitting "a terrible flash of fire, accompanied by a dense cloud of smoke and a noise I can compare to nothing but thunder". In the tale, the electric telegraph is illustrated by a man who "had cultivated his voice to so great an extent that he could have made himself heard from one end of the earth to the other", and the daguerreotype by a man who "directed the sun to paint his portrait".

The early 19th century saw many scientific breakthroughs – Dalton's atomic theory of 1808; Davy's discoveries in electro-chemistry using the battery or 'pile' which Volta had invented in 1799; Faraday's discoveries of the relationship between electricity and magnetism; Lyell's geological synthesis; and Darwin's theory of evolution. But there were other triumphs – both minor and major – and many false starts, as amateur scientists across Europe and America conducted their own experiments and propounded their own theories.

All these discoveries in science – or 'natural philosophy' as it was called – excited enormous public interest. Scientific journals had wide readerships, and lectures attracted large audiences. When Sir Charles Lyell lectured in Bath on local geology in 1846, for example, the 2,000-seat theatre was packed, while over 4,000 attended the annual meetings of the British Association for the Advancement of Science, one of the many new scientific associations that sprang up.

Scientific slide and magic lantern shows, public experiments and evenings round the microscope became highly fashionable entertainment. When the zoologist Sir Richard Owen went to dinner with the English

Sources and Inspiration

Prime Minister Robert Peel, he took his microscope along, and, at the end of the meal, the guests gathered round to examine the remains of the joint in an attempt to discover 'why cold beef sometimes shines like mother-of-pearl when cut'. George Eliot's companion George Lewes recommended the microscope as a cure for bereavement, commenting that after his pet fish died, 'I grieved for him, and, as a consolation, dissected him . . . I had lost a pet, and gained a "preparation".'

All kinds of 'scientific' spectacles were established, and many a fashionable lady and gentleman spent a happy afternoon strolling around the new planetariums, the botanical gardens and a variety of museums, commenting knowledgeably on the exhibits – few Victorian ladies could not name at least 20 species of ferns and fungi. And in the new Regent's Park in London, people flocked to the Diorama, where Daguerre brilliantly recreated illusions of erupting volcanoes and wild storms.

At the heart of this scientific interest was a passion for natural history reflected by the thousands of country gentlemen who went out collecting specimens and making observations. Many kept nature diaries, emulating the 18th-century vicar of Selborne in Hampshire, Gilbert White, whose published journals were perennially popular. Others, such as the raffish French-Creole artist Jean Jacques Audubon and the cool, gentle English eccentric Edward Lear, made beautiful paintings of the species they observed in travels or in their native countryside.

John Martin: The Great Day of His Wrath, Tate Gallery, London

U. PARENT

There was a sense of reverence for Nature, as the titles of the popular natural history books such as *The Marvels of Pond-Life* and *The Wonders of the Sea-Shore* reveal. And in the poetry of the Romantic poets, such as Wordsworth and Keats, this reverence became part of a profound belief in the spiritual bond between humans and Nature.

Interestingly, as the revolution in industry and technology harnessed steam to make ever more powerful engines and machines, so poets and scientists alike became increasingly fascinated by the power of natural phenomena, and the extremes of Nature. Weather sta-

Power and glory
(above) John Martin's vision of the wrath of God is typical of an age transfixed by natural power – phenomena described by the prosaic scientist Faraday as 'The awful conflagration, the vivid lightning flash, the mighty tidal sweep! . . .'

Ann Ronan Picture Library

The eruption of Vesuvius *(right) Many scientists and artists braved fiery ash and lava to witness the successive eruptions of Mount Vesuvius in Italy at first hand.*

Davy in his laboratory
(above left) Electricity was the most thrilling discovery of the age, and many people become obsessed with the idea of releasing its potential. The great scientist Sir Humphrey Davy, friend of the poet Coleridge, was able to make crucial advances in chemistry by harnessing the electric power of the newly invented battery.

Giraudon/Bridgeman Art Library

tions perched on top of bleak mountain tops became the lonely castles of the age, and many men braved the elements to witness at first hand the ferocity of a tempest, the savage power of a glacier, the eruption of a volcano, or the violence of a whirlpool. Such phenomena recur throughout the literature of the day, described with almost breathless awe – nowhere so effectively as in Poe's *A Descent into the Maelstrom*.

The chilly wastes of the polar regions in particular seemed to hold a peculiar power over the imagination, and many explorers set off on voyages of discovery to the Arctic and Antarctic, facing conditions of terrible

fact that many scientists did take considerable risks in experimenting on themselves only served to underline this image. Poe's *Adventures of One Hans Pfall* is an outrageous spoof of a balloon journey to the moon, but the details recall a genuinely courageous experimental balloon ascent in 1804, when the French physicist Gay-Lussac went up to 23,000 feet, and almost froze to death in the process, to test for variations in the composition of the atmosphere.

INSIDE THE MIND

Self-experimentation often meant the scientist using his mind as well as his body. Here the scientist met the poet, and it is typical of the age that the brilliant young scientist Humphrey Davy and the equally brilliant poet Samuel Taylor Coleridge should experiment together with the intoxicating effects of nitrous oxide ('laughing gas'), hoping to unlock some of the secrets of the mind – and perhaps gain some insight into the nature of existence. It is also typical of the age that while Davy wrote poetry, Coleridge maintained a burning interest in science. And the poet Wordsworth imagined a time when the Poet would . . . 'be ready to follow the steps of the Man of Science'.

Yet there was a certain terror, as well as awe, in the knowledge and power that might be wielded by the Man of Science – and a hint that the pursuit of scientific knowledge might be as corrupting as eating from the Tree of Knowledge. The idea of the scientist as Faust, who sells his soul to the Devil for knowledge, recurs

'Animal magnetism'
(below) The possibility that hypnosis could unlock the secrets of the unconscious mind fascinated Poe, who wrote three of his best tales on the subject. But because it was easy to fake, hypnotism acquired a dubious reputation.

hardship. All too often these Arctic explorers perished, and their cold, lonely deaths seemed to haunt the minds of men like Poe. In *The Narrative of Arthur Gordon Pym*, the story ends with the explorer tumbling into a crevasse on the ice, and, during his final illness in 1849, Poe kept crying the name of 'Reynolds!', possibly the polar explorer J.R. Reynolds.

The scientist-explorer, struggling against the elements in the Arctic or the Amazon, was a heroic figure for many of Poe's contemporaries. But so too was the experimental scientist, often working alone in his silent laboratory to unlock the secrets of Nature. The

The northern lights
(above) Voyagers to the Arctic were filled with wonder at the beauty of the aurora borealis, while scientists at home were convinced of the link between light and magnetism. But it was only in the 20th century that it could be proved that the aurora is the result of this relationship.

in the writing of the age, notably in Mary Shelley's horror story *Frankenstein*, and in Poe's tales. The philosopher Thomas Carlyle felt the same devilishness even in the power of steam, comparing a train journey to 'Faust's flight on the Devil's mantle'.

Nowhere was the scientist's potential power more awesome, or even more terrifying, than in the field of electro-magnetism. The harnessing of the power of electricity was among the most thrilling spectacles of the age. Ever since Benjamin Franklin had sent up a kite to catch electricity in the late 18th century, people had been obsessed by the idea. The poet Shelley tried to repeat Franklin's experiment to produce 'the most stupendous results', while after Volta had invented his pile (battery) in 1799, scientists flung themselves into the competition to build even bigger and more powerful ones.

THE POWER OF LIFE

What was especially exciting, and dangerous, about electricity was that it seemed to be the very spark of life. It was after all Galvani's experiments on dead frogs' legs, twitching under the influence of an electric current, that had led directly to Volta's invention of the pile. Many people genuinely believed that galvanization – applying electric power to a corpse – could bring it back to life, and experiments continued throughout the first half of the 19th century. Power over life and death was a devastating prospect for the human race, as Mary Shelley showed in the moral dilemmas of *Frankenstein* – and Poe made fun of in *Some Words with a Mummy*.

The allied force of magnetism might be equally fundamental to life – though the direct relationship between electricity and magnetism was not appreciated until Faraday's experiments in the 1820s – and thousands of magnetic stations were set up to map the earth's magnetic field. The experiments led to wider speculation on the subject – 'Animal magnetism', which was the original name given to hypnosis, was apparently the most fascinating manifestation of the psychic power of magnetism.

Hypnosis had been discovered by the Austrian Anton Mesmer in the late 18th century and, because no-one could adequately explain 'mesmerism', it acquired a rather dubious reputation, particularly as it was often practised by complete frauds. Yet just as with opium, the possibility that mesmerism could provide real insights into the nature of the 'spiritual universe' meant that it held a continuing interest for many poets and writers.

Bulwer Lytton's *A Strange Story* is about mesmerism; so too are three of Poe's tales: *A Tale of the Ragged Mountains*, *Mesmeric Revelation*, and *The Facts in the Case of M. Valdemar*. Poe read extensively and voraciously on the subject, advocating anyone interested to read Chauncey Hare Townshend's *Facts in Mesmerism*, which gave him the detailed case histories on which his own mesmeric tales are based. *The Facts in the Case of M. Valdemar* is told so convincingly that many people believed Poe was reporting a true case. For in an age when new scientific discoveries were daily expanding the bounds of knowledge, anything – however strange – must have seemed possible.

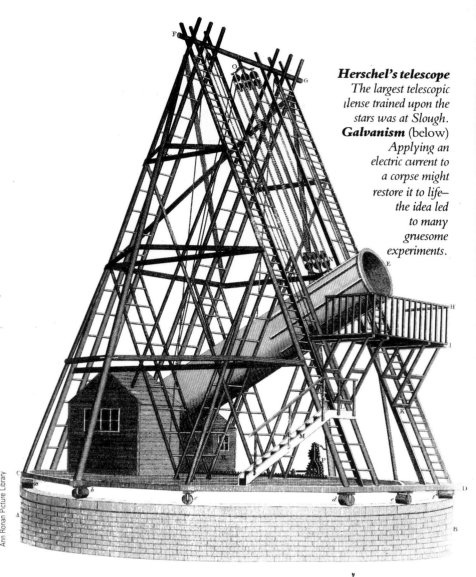

Herschel's telescope
The largest telescopic lense trained upon the stars was at Slough.
Galvanism *(below)*
Applying an electric current to a corpse might restore it to life– the idea led to many gruesome experiments.

Polar exploration
(below) James Ross' expedition to the Arctic, in 1831, was one of many voyages to the Poles, with their 'stupendous ramparts of ice', that haunted Poe's imagination and inspired his writing.

WILKIE COLLINS

1824-1889

When Wilkie Collins paused in the telling of his latest thriller, Victorian England held its breath. His heroines were the talk of every parlour, and success drew a cloak around the celebrity's highly unconventional private life. A colossus, twinned with Dickens, his was the art not of caricature but of intricate plot, plausible villain, spine-chilling encounter, heart-stopping shock. But perhaps the brooding fears which menace his characters convince his readers because such torments surrounded Collins himself.

Runaway Success

Wilkie Collins wrote prodigiously, took on two common-law wives, fathered three illegitimate children, and made a fortune. In his life as in his work he was a 'Master of Sensation'.

William Wilkie Collins was the firstborn son of William Collins, a successful landscape artist and Royal Academician. Like his father, Wilkie was to be a part of the circle of writers and painters of his day, but that was where the similarity ended. The elder William Collins was a blinkered, tight-fisted Victorian, espousing the beliefs and morality of the Church of England and the Tory party. The younger William Collins was a radical freethinker, and brazenly flaunted his disdain for the conventions of the day throughout his life.

Wilkie was born on 8 January 1824 in a small house in Hampstead, north London. Probably due to some accident at birth, Wilkie's left temple was depressed while his right one bulged. As an adult this, together with a disproportionately large head, short stature (5 feet 6 inches), acute short-sightedness and unusually small hands and feet, gave him an extremely odd appearance.

When Wilkie was six, the family moved to more spacious accommodation in Bayswater from where Wilkie, three years later, was sent to Maida Hill Academy, an exclusive private school. Here, though not far from home, he boarded. Like many imaginative and intelligent boys, he hated school.

TOUR OF ITALY

Already possessed of a strong will, Wilkie was 'perpetually getting punished as a bad boy'. Yet his proficiency led to accusations of being a teacher's pet, and he was frequently bullied and thrashed by the bigger boys. But at the age of 14 his father took him, together with the rest of the family, to Italy. They stayed six months, and the experience for Wilkie was decisive. 'I learnt more which has since been of use to me among the pictures, the scenery, and the people', he recalled later, 'than I ever learnt at school.'

At the age of 17 he left Maida Hill with no clear idea of what he was going to do. Oxford was considered by his father but, to Wilkie's relief, rejected when the cost was calculated. While the family debated what he should do, Wilkie spent his first summer of freedom roaming round the countryside that then bordered north London. As recalled in the semi-autobiographical *A Rogue's Life,* he met 'horsemen in hunting fields', chatted 'amicably with tinkers in ditches. . .pedlars, tramps and labourers. . .all. . .were alike to [his] cosmopolitan sympathies'.

What Wilkie wanted was a life of excitement and adventure, 'a good berth in the merchant navy. . .or an exploring expedition to Australia'. But after rows with his father and empty threats to run away, he settled for a desk job at Antrobus & Co., the London tea brokers.

William Collins, RA
Charles Collins captured the image of his father (left) on paper in 1846; his brother Wilkie was to do the same two years later in a celebrated biography.

National Portrait Gallery

Boyhood portrait
An early portrait of Wilkie by his father. William Collins named his son after his friend and colleague Sir David Wilkie. It is perhaps ironic that it was his second son, Charles, who was to achieve fame as an artist rather than Wilkie.

His sole diversion during this time was the 'brilliant land of glitter and glass' of London's West End. It was a vicarious pleasure he enjoyed, too poor on a clerk's pay to buy anything more than an occasional cheap cigar. Walking home after his 'nine hours of the most ungrateful daily labour' he sat in his bedroom almost every night and wrote.

Exactly when he formed the ambition to become a writer is not known. But by the age of 19 he was turning out romantic and melodramatic stories for the penny-novel journals. None of these early efforts of his

Hampstead Heath
(left) Wilkie's first home made a lasting impression on him. In The Woman in White *it forms the dramatic backdrop to the equally dramatic encounter.*

Courtroom drama
Wilkie never practised as a barrister, but he studied Law and was fascinated by the subject. He based The Woman in White *on an earlier French lawsuit.*

seem to have survived, but as Professor Nuel Davis, Collins' biographer, suggests, they were undoubtedly 'trash'.

Increasingly, writing became his real interest. In the imagined scenes he created night after night he lived a life denied him at Antrobus & Co. Utterly determined, ignoring countless rejections, he finally wrote a story in 1843, *The Last Stagecoachman*, worthy of the pages of *The Illuminated Journal*. Encouraged by its editor Douglas Jerrold, Collins began a novel. Set in Tahiti, it was an improbable story of love and intrigue. Undaunted by its failure to find a publisher, he began another, a story of ancient Rome called *Antonina*.

It took Collins some seven years to complete *Antonina*. In 1846, on seeing just a part of it his father was sufficiently impressed by Wilkie's intellectual ability to release him from Antrobus & Co. and enter his name on to the rolls of Lincoln's Inn.

The law held no more interest for Wilkie as an occupation than did tea, and there is no evidence that he ever studied it with a view to practising. Content to live at home and write, he ate the required number of dinners and in due course was called to the Bar.

But it was his father's death in 1847 that was to change his life. One of the last requests of William Collins was that his eldest son should write his biography. Despite the hostility that had existed between them, Wilkie accepted the commission and wrote a dutiful, competent, *Memoir*. 'An author I was to be,' he said, 'and an author I became in 1848.'

Though not a commercial success, the book brought Wilkie to the attention of the critics – mainly family friends – who wrote encouragingly of his abilities as an author. With £100 pocketed from sales of the book he went to Paris where, apart from completing *Antonina*, he discovered an appetite for dry champagne, French cuisine and prostitutes.

Key Dates

1824 born in London

1847 father dies

1848 first book, *The Memoirs of William Collins RA* published

1851 meets Charles Dickens

1854 encounter with Caroline Graves

1860 *The Woman in White* published

1868 mother dies. Caroline Graves marries. Becomes involved with Martha Rudd. *The Moonstone* published

1870 Dickens dies

1871 reunited with Caroline Graves

1873 reading tour of the United States

1889 dies in London

The Writer's Life

Home was now 38 Blandford Square, London, to which his mother had moved after the death of her husband. Here with his younger brother Charley, already a recognized artist, he met publishers, writers and the two leading pre-Raphaelite painters, William Holman Hunt and John Everett Millais. With the publication of *Antonina* (1850), through the efforts of John Ruskin, Collins became an accepted author leading a comfortable, sheltered life in his mother's house.

Seeing himself as a producer of saleable commodities for a commercial market, books followed in swift succession. *Rambles Beyond Railways* was written after trudging 238 miles around Cornwall accompanied by an artist named Blandling who illustrated the book. A second novel, *Basil,* was begun, and a play, *A Court Duel,* written and produced at Miss Kelly's Theatre, Soho. His short stories appeared in Bentley's *Miscellany* – one of the leading periodicals of the day.

Still only 27, Collins had good reason to appear confidently pleased with himself. But it was his meeting with Charles Dickens on 12 March 1851 in the rooms of John Forster, that was to prove the most important encounter of his life, both as a writer and as a man.

Dickens was 12 years his senior. In him Collins recognized a tireless nervous energy that matched his own, an inexhaustible and stimulating creativity, and a man who at the age of 40 had a similar penchant for the seamy side of life. Together they formed a friendship which, if lacking in emotional warmth – Collins himself was an undemonstrative, rather tepid man – gave each the confidence to flout the conventions of a society they both, at heart, despised.

Wining and dining at fashionable West End restau-

THE WOMAN IN WHITE

John Everett Millais
(above) The artist was with Collins and his brother Charles on the fateful summer's evening when they encountered the 'Woman in White'. Wilkie was so moved by this that he charged after her, into the night, to discover her secret.

It was after a dinner party in July 1854 that an event took place which was to change the course of Wilkie's life and inspire his greatest work. Wilkie was accompanying the painter Millais back to his studio when, according to Millais' son, they suddenly heard 'a piercing scream coming from the garden of a villa. . . . While pausing to consider what to do, the iron gate leading to the garden was dashed open, and from it came the figure of a young and very beautiful woman dressed in flowing white robes that shone in the moonlight.'

The mysterious woman was 20-year-old Caroline Graves. From this strange beginning, she was to fall in love with Collins and live with him for most of his life.

Venetian travels

In 1853 Wilkie embarked on a two-month tour of Italy with Dickens and Augustus Egg. They took in all the major sights and of his stay in Venice he wrote to his mother 'We lead the most luxurious, dandy-dilettante sort of life here. Our gondola . . . waits on us wherever we go. We live among pictures and palaces all day, and among Operas, Ballets and Cafes more than half the night.'

'Master of Sensation'

Wilkie once complained that Nature had got him 'all out of drawing' and this somewhat cruel cartoon by Adriano Cecioni captures his disproportionately large head in relation to his small body and spindly legs. It appeared in Vanity Fair *in 1872 when the author would have been just 48 and shows how gout and illness had prematurely aged him.*

patronage of Dickens, Collins prospered to a degree that was to equal and eventually exceed that of the master himself. Financial independence also set him free from the stifling conventions he so despised. A radical freethinker, his sympathy for the casualties of Victorian England took on an increasingly socialistic hue as he grew older. And in his personal life he went even further in his defiance of accepted social mores than Dickens ever dared.

From 1854, after his dramatic encounter one July evening with the beautiful Mrs Caroline Graves, he set up house with her and her baby daughter Lizzie, though he retained a nominal address at his mother's.

Whatever view society took of Collins' relationship with Caroline Graves, it was one which was to last until the end of his life. He missed her terribly in the periods when they were separated and, as he wrote in *The Queen of Hearts,* he was "a man bewitched". In *The Frozen Deep* he described how on their very first meeting "when she embraced me, her arms folded round me like the wings of an angel".

Caroline would have been happy to marry Collins. He, however, never showed the slightest inclination to do so. When his mother died in 1868 (she was always thought to be a barrier to their marriage), Caroline issued Wilkie with an ultimatum, in effect, 'marry me or I'll marry Mr Clow' (a plumber whom she had met when he carried out some work in their home).

'Wilkie's affairs defy all prediction,' Dickens wrote to his sister-in-law Georgina, 'For anything one knows, the whole matrimonial pretence may be a lie of that woman's.' It was not, however, and on 4 October 1868 Caroline married Mr Clow with Wilkie in attendance.

rants, they shared a passion for the theatre which resulted in many joint private performances, attended music halls and planned nights of 'dissipation', behaving in each other's company, 'like Don Giovanni' as Dickens described it. Whether this included visits to brothels in London is unknown, but they certainly frequented such establishments when travelling together on the Continent.

Impressed by the younger man's literary abilities, Dickens took Collins under his wing. Commissioning articles and short stories for his own weekly *Household Words,* he advised the less experienced Wilkie on how to handle wily publishers in that most delicate of matters, money. A willing and accomplished pupil, Collins soon mastered this art and was able to command a handsome return for his work.

TRAVELS WITH DICKENS

In October 1853, Dickens and Collins made their first trip abroad together with the artist Augustus Egg. The 'holiday' was a gruelling itinerary taking in almost every city and sight between Boulogne and Rome and back. Always physically weak, Collins could not keep up with Dickens. He sprained an ankle early in the trip, and rode on a donkey while Dickens strode ahead on foot. Collins' purse also proved unequal to Dickens' inexhaustible extravagance. Staying only at the best hotels and consuming nothing but the choicest food and wine, Collins returned to London in debt.

The debts, however, were short-lived. Under the

CHARITABLE ACTS

Among the many affinities that Wilkie Collins and Dickens shared was a love of theatre. Together they saw performances, planned and wrote plays, and ultimately acted side-by-side in their own creations.

In 1851 Dickens formed the Guild of Art and Literature, an organization which put on plays to raise money for needy authors and artists. Its aims were 'to render such assistance to both as shall never compromise their independence; and to found a few Institutions where honourable rest from arduous labour shall still be associated with the discharge of congenial duties.'

Not so Bad as We Seem by Bulwer-Lytton was their first comedy, and Dickens subsequently wrote to its author that 'Wilkie fell upon his new part with great alacrity and heartiness', and to his wife Dickens wrote 'Collins was *admirable* — got up excellently, played throughly well, and missed nothing.' The production, which had its debut in London before touring the provinces, raised a staggering £4,000 for the Guild.

The Frozen Deep *by Wilkie was a stirring play about heroism, sex and sacrifice set in the North Pole. Starring Dickens (below) and Wilkie – each sporting nine months' growth of beard – it was a brilliant vehicle for their talents.*

One reason for Collins' apparent indifference to Caroline's marriage was that he had taken up with the "fine-fleshy beef-fed English girl" (as he describes her in *The Fallen Leaves*), Martha Rudd. Nine months to the very day after Caroline's wedding, Martha gave birth to a daughter, Marian. But with Caroline's marriage failing, she was back with Wilkie in the summer of 1871, soon after the birth of Wilkie's second daughter by Martha Rudd. From then on Collins' visits to Martha became very infrequent, although a third child, a boy, was born in 1875.

Collins' unusual private life did nothing to diminish his popularity. His earnings for the time were phenomenal. For a novel of which he had not written a word he was paid an advance of 5000 guineas in 1862. And in the year ending September 1863 his earnings topped £10,000 – probably more than any other writer earned in a single year in the 19th century.

RACKED WITH PAIN

But behind the appearance of a successful, self-assured author, Wilkie Collins suffered torments in mind and body. He could be a tiresome hypochondriac, and fussy about his personal comfort and well being. But from the age of 30, he suffered from what was medically defined as 'rheumatic gout'. It first attacked his eyes so that, as one observer remarked, they became 'bags of blood'. The disease spread to his knees and feet, and he was a virtual invalid for the last 20 years of his life, spending long periods confined to bed. There, surrounded by bottles, potions and tablets, he continued to work indefatigably.

To the gout was added neuralgia, rheumatism, arthritis and insomnia. There is a tendency to think that these afflictions were psychosomatic in origin, and it seems that each attack was preceded by a bout of intense

New York harbour

(above right) Wilkie sailed into New York on 25 Sept 1873 at the start of his American lecture tour. He enjoyed it but complained of autograph hunters and female reporters. Although he must have taken some pleasure in his fame, he felt that he could well have done without the embraces of 'the oldest and ugliest' of the female reporters.

'Divine laundanum'

(left) Prescribed laudanum as a painkiller, Collins took it in ever-increasing doses, occasionally seeing a green woman with tusk teeth lying in wait for him. Apparently when his manservant George Hellow consumed just half of his master's dose, he died almost instantly.

Kensal Rise Cemetery

Collins' burial in Sept 1889 was a simple affair in accordance with his wishes. Caroline Graves was buried at his side in 1895 and Martha Rudd, his other 'wife', tended the grave until her own death a year later.

morbid depression. But the origins of the illness did nothing to diminish the appalling pain Collins had to contend with almost daily. Trying almost every known remedy (principally colchicum and morphine) and engaging a succession of eminent physicians and quacks, he eventually found relief in 'divine laudanum'.

Of the many novels, short stories and plays he continued to pour out with unceasing application, none show quite so clearly his addiction to laudanum as *The Moonstone*. Serialized in Dickens' literary magazine *All the Year Round,* its strange, eerie effect was undoubtedly drug-induced. It was written while his mother lay dying in an adjacent room suffering from the last stages of senile dementia, while he himself suffered the ravages of gout. 'In the intervals of grief, in the intermissions of pain', he said of this time, 'I dictated from my bed. . . *The Moonstone.*'

This novel marked the high point of Collins' literary career. Though he continued to publish novels, short stories and plays at an extraordinary rate, his reputation

among the critics, never high at the best of times, slumped. Even his loyal supporter Dickens became disenchanted with him for a while, commenting on *The Moonstone* that 'the construction was beyond endurance'. But by 1868 the two men had re-established friendly relations and Dickens' death in 1870 lost Collins his closest friend, one who had in many ways mirrored his own view of literature and society.

In 1873-4, Collins embarked on a reading tour of the United States, following once again in Dickens' footsteps. Although it was greeted with warmth and kindness it was not the financial success he had hoped for, due almost entirely to his poor reading ability.

Now an overweight, wheezing, stooped little man with round spectacles and a flowing white beard, the last 15 years of his life were spent with Caroline and her daughter Lizzie (who became his secretary), writing and fighting daily against pain and drug addiction.

Still popular with the public – the only yardstick he considered worthwhile – he was almost entirely forgotten and neglected by the literary establishment. Few critics even knew he was still alive, and for years Collins worried about reading of his death in a newspaper.

Alone in his gas-lit study writing serials, he gradually sank into delirium, believing himself to be pursued by a green woman with tusk teeth. On mounting the staircase on his way to bed, he imagined her biting a chunk out of his shoulder.

On 23 September 1889, after suffering a heart attack, Wilkie Collins wrote a last note to his long-suffering physician Frank Beard, 'I am dying – come if you can'. At 10.35 that morning, aged 65, he died. Following his instructions, he was buried without ceremony in a common plot at Kensal Green Cemetery, London. When Caroline Graves died six years later in 1895, she was buried beside him.

THE WOMAN IN WHITE

A melodrama with a difference, Collins' masterpiece pits the vulnerable and the good against the fiendish machinations of two kinds of villain.

Collins' most popular novel, *The Woman in White* is a compellingly readable thriller. The suspense is sustained by an exquisitely managed plot, which frequently seems about to reach an unavoidably unhappy end only to re-open just when the reader has given up hope. The first mysterious appearance of the woman dressed in white is one of the most dramatic passages in English literature. Collins' classic mystery hinges around "the idea of a conspiracy. . .to rob a woman of her identity by confounding her with another woman, sufficiently like her in personal appearance to answer the wicked purpose". The story of this ingenious crime is told by a series of key witnesses: "As a Judge might once have heard it, so the Reader shall hear it now. No circumstance of importance . . . shall be related on hearsay evidence."

GUIDE TO THE PLOT

Walter Hartright, a young London drawing master, has been engaged by Frederick Fairlie Esquire of Limmeridge House, Cumberland, to instruct two young ladies in watercolour painting. After a farewell evening with his family, Walter walks back into London. As he crosses Hampstead Heath, he feels a ghostly touch upon his shoulder: he is confronted by a distressed woman dressed entirely in white. She has "not exactly the manner of a lady, and, at the same time, not the manner of a woman in the humblest rank of life". Someone is chasing her.

As he helps her evade her pursuers, Walter learns that she lives in fear of a certain baronet. By a remarkable coincidence, she also has happy recollections of his destination, Limmeridge House.

Arriving at Limmeridge, Walter meets his pupils, Marian Halcombe and her half-sister Laura Fairlie, for the first time. Though not pretty, the dark-haired Marian is warm, witty and intelligent, while the musically gifted Laura is a "fair, delicate girl" with whom Walter instantly falls in love. Their guardian (Walter's employer) Frederick Fairlie is a "languidly fretful" hypochondriac.

Laura (who bears an uncanny resemblance to the woman in white) returns Walter's romantic feelings, but is bound by a deathbed pledge to her late father to marry Sir Percival Glyde of Blackwater Park in Hampshire. A "sharp autumn breeze" scatters the leaves at Walter's feet as he hears this news. But he behaves honourably, and the sympathetic Marian arranges for him to leave Limmeridge House prematurely. His thoughts still running on Laura, he sets off as an artist with an archaeological expedition to Central America in the hope of forgetting her.

Laura Fairlie duly becomes Lady Glyde. But as Sir Percival's financial position worsens, he becomes more and more obviously interested in his new wife's money. He also has a guilty secret shared only by a certain Mrs Catherick and her daughter.

With her callous mother's approval, Anne Catherick has been locked up in a mental asylum by Sir Percival to ensure her silence. That same Anne is the woman in white. When Percival hears of her escape, he panics.

When Count Fosco, Laura's uncle, arrives with his wife at Blackwater Park, even the shrewd Marian is impressed by him. But she soon finds out that the seemingly charming Count is a party to Sir Percival Glyde's wicked schemes. He also stands to gain if she dies childless. The two men succeed in getting Laura committed to the asylum, passing her off as the escaped Anne Catherick. The real Anne dies and is buried at Limmeridge – but under the name of Laura Glyde.

Marian, meanwhile, lies gravely ill, unaware of what is happening to her sister. When she recovers, Marian's suspicions are alerted when she discovers that a mental patient, 'Anne Catherick', is suffering from the delusion that she is Lady Glyde. Marian braves the asylum, recognizes Laura, and bribes a nurse

> *"What had I done? Assisted the victim of the most horrible of all false imprisonments to escape; or cast loose on the wide world of London an unfortunate creature whose actions it was my duty . . . mercifully to control?"*

A gloomy setting
(left) Darkness and gloom shrouds the occupants of Blackwater Park. It contributes to the black-hearted menace which awaits Laura Fairlie there.

Accomplishment
Laura at the piano (right) spoke volumes to Victorian readers to whom a sweet voice and lightness of touch meant a pure soul. By contrast, Count Fosco's "bass voice thundered out the notes".

B.W. Leader 'A Lonely Grange'. Fine Art Photographic Library

A.J. Woolmer 'The Evening Hymn'. City of York Art Gallery/Bridgeman Art Library

Airy lightness
(left) The prospect, the architecture and the gardens of Limmeridge House are in keeping with the nature of the women who live there. The place makes the same pleasant impression on the hero as it has on the besieged and troubled mind of the unhappy Anne Catherick.

A woman in white
(right) Carrying implications of virginity, innocence and ghostliness on which Collins capitalizes, "Like a Shadow she first came . . . in the loneliness of the night. Like a Shadow she passes away . . ." But foremost in the writer's mind may have been his true-life encounter with a figure, all in white, late one summer evening – a woman who changed his life.

T. Couture 'La Grande Duchesse de Baden'. (Detail) Palais de Compiegne/Photo Hutin

to release her. Meanwhile, Walter Hartright has arrived back in England. Hearing of the death of 'Lady Glyde', he goes to Limmeridge to pay his respects at her grave. At sunset, two women approach the graveyard. One is Marian – the other, his beloved Laura.

Together the three set out to foil the evil plans hatched at Blackwater Park. The discovery of Sir Percival's dark secret is a beginning. But the discovery has fatal consequences. For beyond Percival looms the far more formidable Count Fosco – an "irresistible" man lacking in all moral scruple.

SOPHISTICATED MELODRAMA

Wilkie Collins' novel is a melodrama, a struggle between good and evil, with a happy ending. 'Melodrama', one of the most popular forms of Victorian entertainment, promised a clash between hero and villain, a series of sensational events testing the hero to the full, and a heart-warming ending. But *The Woman in White* has little in common with the absurd plots, crude characters, and implausible action familiar to Victorian theatre-goers.

Walter Hartright is an innocent man; Laura Fairlie is a lovely, defenceless woman; Sir Percival Glyde is a wicked squire; Count Fosco is the archetypal aristocratic, foreign villain. But each of these conventional characters has a psychological depth admirably explored by the 'witness-in-the-dock' structure. We come to know them as characters far too complex to be readily labelled 'bad' or 'good'.

The character of Fosco, for instance, does not observe the unwritten law of melodrama that the arch villain should be thin and sharp-featured. Fat and swarming with white pet mice, he is rendered bad by association: "the sight of them creeping about a man's body is for some reason not pleasant to me. It . . . suggests hideous ideas of men dying in prison with the crawling creatures of the dungeon preying on them undisturbed."

Reader's Guide

Fosco's affection for his animals even lends him a humanity which lowers the reader's guard and sets us wondering if such a man can be all bad: "it was impossible to resist the comical distress of so very large a man at the loss of so very small a mouse".

As with modern pantomimes, Victorian melodramas included comic characters for light relief. Collins' humorous characters certainly entertain (chiefly by his witty descriptions of them). Of Mrs Vesey he writes: "some of us rush through life, and some of us saunter through life. Mrs Vesey *sat* through life." But she and Professor Pesca, Frederick Fairlie and Mrs Michelson are all well integrated into the plot and move the action forward rather than holding it up.

> "*Vast perspectives of success unroll themselves before my eyes. I accomplish my destiny with a calmness which is terrible to myself.*"

All the events in *The Woman in White* are anchored in reality rather than resulting from implausible flights of imagination and fancy. The initial encounter between Walter and the woman in white was inspired by Collins' own dramatic meeting one night with his lover-to-be, Caroline Graves. And he based Fosco's plot against Laúra on a sensational 18th-century French lawsuit. (The structure itself was calculated to gratify the Victorian appetite for verbatim newspaper reports of extraordinary and lurid trials.)

THRILLS AND REVELATIONS

Serialization in a weekly magazine demanded that the author maintain a high pitch of excitement and keep the thrills and revelations coming thick and fast. Although Collins purported never to give the least consideration to the periodical format, Dickens himself congratulated him on his proficiency: "it grips the difficulties of the weekly portion and throws them in a masterly style".

Sometimes the 'cliff-hangers' are at moments of high excitement – such as the unexplained arrival in the churchyard of the 'dead' Laura. But rather than pitch the reader, at very even intervals, into scenes of danger or discovery, other episodes end at a seemingly tame moment. But even tame moments are weighted with menace by some subtle mention of the weather:

*the summer silence was broken by the shuddering of a low, melancholy wind among the trees. We all felt the sudden chill in the atmosphere; but the Count was the first to notice the stealthy rising of the wind. He stopped while he was lighting my candle for me, and held up his hand warningly: 'Listen!' he said.
. . . . be a change to-morrow.'*"

Betrayed by illness
(right) Marian Halcombe discovers the evil conspiracy between Count Fosco and Percival Glyde only to become so ill that she is helpless to hinder them. Her collapse also allows her diary to fall into the hands of an ardent but deadly admirer.

Moonlight illuminates
(below) Two crucial scenes take place at night. The first is the encounter with the woman in white; the second culminates in a just reckoning for her tormentor. Part of the book's delight arises from the 'twinning' of events and characters.

Unfair influences
The title page illustration of the first edition of The Woman in White *(above) shows the coercion brought to bear on Laura to make her sign away her property. Glyde is tactless and unsubtle, Fosco a far more insinuating persecutor.*

In the Background

BROTHERHOOD OF COUSINS

U ntil its unification, Italy was a welter of states, some ruled by tyrants such as Ferdinand IV of Naples and Sicily. Republican undercurrents were seething, however. Secret societies formed to foment rebellion – notably the Carbonari, who called each other 'cousin'. Members risked arrest (below) and death. The Brotherhood of the novel is plainly styled on this society.

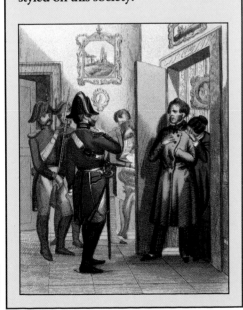

The multiple-viewpoint method of telling the story allows new revelations to unfold from the depositions of each new witness. No all-seeing author is present to warn the reader against the villains. We shiver at the discovery that Fosco has read through Marian's diary, as Marian's writing peters out and is followed by Fosco's own, blithely menacing postscript.

Walter's encounter with a sweetheart he believes to be dead is turned into something much more than a happy, sentimental shock: we share his spiralling terror at a series of supernatural impressions. When Collins wanted to grip his readers, he applied all the artistry of a writer of horror stories:

"the veiled woman had possession of me, body and soul. . .We stood face to face with the tombstone between us. She was close to the inscription on the side of the pedestal. Her gown touched the black letters.

The voice came nearer, and rose and rose more passionately still. 'Hide your face! don't look at her! Oh, for God's sake, spare him –'
The woman lifted her veil."

PAIRS AND CONTRASTS

Nature and the weather are in sympathy with the action of the story. The day of Laura's wedding dawns "wild unsettled". The graveyard at Limmeridge is bathed in a spectacular sunset when Walter is reunited with her. This is a familiar device, and nothing new to Collins. But it serves to heighten the deliberate contrasts built into the book.

The two settings, Limmeridge House and Blackwater Park, take on active roles in the plot. They are good and evil embodied. The home of the Fairlie family is a light, beautiful place. When Walter looked out of his window there, "the sea opened before me joyously under the broad August sunlight". Limmeridge has "many windows", and glass doors are thrown open to reveal "a profusion of flowers". Even the grounds are not bounded by a forbidding fence but by "high white walls". By contrast, Blackwater Park is "dead flat", "almost suffocated" by trees which look "dimly black and solid in the distance, like a great wall of rock". The house itself is dusty and damp, full of hideous family portraits. The stagnant lake which gives it its name is "just the place for a murder".

Almost every character in the book has a contrasting 'counterpart' of some kind. It would be a trite device if this were simply a way of helping us to 'take sides', but it is much more subtle than that. Marian is dark and unattractive in comparison with Laura, but this hint to distrust her is, in itself, misleading. What, and who, can be trusted?

This pairing of counterparts gives the book a deeply intriguing 'double ration' of characters and plot – and continually reminds us of further unforeseen possibilities. There are two houses, two heroines, two villains, two graveyard revelations, two women who share one face. All these 'paired' people and events enrich the fabric of the plot and remove it several paces from simple melodrama. The author also convinces the reader that, when all has been revealed and the distrust ends, he has well and truly had his money's worth.

CHARACTERS IN FOCUS

The Woman in White contains a deeply satisfying 'double ration' of heroines and villains. The angelic Laura Fairlie has a commendably dogged champion in Walter Hartright, but even he is aided by the "magnificent" Marian Halcombe. Marian is more than a match for the sophisticated evil of Count Fosco, whose malevolence makes the clumsy wickedness of Sir Percival look like child's play. The weak heroine and villain seldom appear alone.

WHO'S WHO

Walter Hartright   Hero and narrator. A young drawing master and "natural" gentleman. His love for Laura is genuine and, when rejected, he acts nobly and selflessly.

Marian Halcombe   Heroine and narrator. Though poor and "ugly", she exudes "grace, wit and high-breeding". She earns Count Fosco's "fatal admiration" and succeeds in saving Laura.

Laura Fairlie   Her fortune makes her the victim of villains. Her "beauty, gentleness and simple truth" inspire the devotion of Walter and Marian.

Sir Percival Glyde   A "weak and shabby" villain who marries Laura. He will stop at nothing to preserve the secret of his past.

Count Fosco   A fat and flamboyant Italian nobleman. His sophisticated criminality is masked by "irresistible" charm and erudition.

Frederick Fairlie   Laura's self-preoccupied and "languidly-fretful" guardian. He does nothing to protect his niece from her persecutors.

Anne Catherick   The woman in white. Fragile but sane, she knows about Sir Percival's secret and bears an uncanny likeness to Laura, both of which make her a victim.

Mrs Catherick   Anne's "heartless" mother. Her collusion with Sir Percival allows him to confine her daughter in a lunatic asylum.

Mrs Clements   Anne's surrogate mother. Her support for the woman in white contrasts with the callousness of Mrs Catherick.

"heartless" Mrs Catherick (left) is driven by consuming ambition for the social status of which she feels she has been robbed. Even though she commits her own daughter to a madhouse, her conscience does not trouble her. "'I have matched the respectable people . . . *The clergyman bows to me!'*" she crows, as though that in itself puts her beyond the reach of retribution.

Christie's/Bridgeman Art Library

Tate Gallery/Bridgeman Art Library

J.S. von Carolsfeld 'Friedrich Oliver Sketching' Albertina, Vienna

"strikingly original and perplexingly contradictory", everything about Isidor Ottavio Baldassare Fosco (left), Count of the Holy Roman Empire, Knight Grand Cross of the Order of the Brazen Crown, disturbs. "Fat as he is, his movements are astonishingly light and easy" – in fact, there is a feminine sensitivity behind "the horrible freshness and cheerfulness and vitality of the man". He is as "nervously sensitive" as his teeming white mice, his cockatoo and his canaries. Yet serene self-confidence, a brilliant intellect and "a daring independence of thought" inflate Fosco to the proportions of a diabolical anti-hero.

The epitome of romantic beauty and the object of Walter's love is Laura Fairlie (right): "everybody thinks her sweet-tempered and charming . . . In short, she is an angel". But there is a simple vulnerability about her which "in a shadowy way, suggested . . . the idea of something wanting". She has moral strength enough to keep her vow to marry Percival Glyde, and to send Walter away ignorant of her love for him. But her abiding role is that of the victim. She can only shelter behind her stronger half-sister and dream wistfully of Walter.

Walter Hartright (above) narrates much of the story: our sympathies are with him because we see the action through his eyes. But others' observations about him leave us in no doubt that here is the hero of the piece. This "modest and gentlemanlike young man" is pleasant and honourable, "the most intelligent and the most attentive" of art masters. But has he the dynamism to foil Fosco or Glyde?

"This magnificent Marian" Halcombe (right) is a source of admiration to hero and villain alike. Despite being "dark and ugly", her grace, intelligence and force of character stir devoted affection in her allies and make her "the first and last weakness of Fosco's life". Nothing but her bravery holds off disaster.

"a most prepossessing man", Percival Glyde creates good initial impressions: "His tact and taste were never at fault". But after his marriage to Laura, a nervous irritability afflicts him – and slowly his inmost heart is laid bare, "black as night; and on it was written in the red flaming letters which are the handwriting of the fallen angel: 'Without pity and without remorse'." Yet under the vast shadow of Count Fosco, Sir Percival shrinks into a nervy, fumbling and inadequate villain.

THRILLING TALES

Collins' skill at depicting colourful, even improbable characters was as well developed as his eye for an intricate plot. His talent made him the most popular and successful writer of his day.

Collins' reputation as the grand master of the Victorian melodramatic thriller rests upon two great masterpieces, *The Woman in White* and *The Moonstone*. The poet and critic T. S. Eliot considered that there was no novelist alive 'who could not learn something from Collins in the art of interesting and exciting the reader'.

Victorian critics were less positive: 'in sliding panels, trap-doors and artificial beards, Mr Collins is nearly as clever as anyone who has ever fried a pancake in a hat', was a typical review of the time. For though the public loved his suspense-ridden, sensational short stories and novels – at the height of his career, he was one of the most famous and successful writers of his day – the press panned him.

One of the main criticisms levelled against Collins was that he concentrated upon constructing complex, ingenious plots at the expense of creating believable characters. His preface to the 1861 edition of *The Woman in White* answers such criticism, and points out that character and plot are inextricably linked: 'I have always held the old-fashioned opinion that the primary object of a work of fiction should be to tell a story. . .The only narrative which can hope to hold the attention of readers is a narrative which interests them about men and women – for the perfectly obvious reason that they are men and women themselves.' The logic seems faultless.

In *The Woman in White* and *The Moonstone*, the main characters – albeit originating from the villain-versus-victim repertoire of stock

Victorian melodrama – are as fascinating and complex as the plots. Count Fosco and Marian are superbly drawn individuals, not standard 'types'. And in *The Moonstone*, the portrait of Sergeant Cuff, the first enigmatic detective in English fiction, is built up, detail upon detail, with devastating precision in the finest traditions of characterization:

He was dressed all in decent black, with a white cravat round his neck. His face was as sharp as a hatchet, and the skin of it was as yellow and dry and withered as an autumn leaf. His eyes, of a steely light grey, had a very disconcerting trick, when they encountered your eyes, of looking as if they expected something more from you than you were aware of yourself. . .He might have been a parson, or an undertaker – or anything else you like, except what he really was.'

But in many of his numerous other novels (of which there are 25 in all), and particularly in his late works, Collins' penchant for complicated, improbable plots is matched by his increasingly bizarre attraction for grotesque and overly caricatured characters. Examples range from a blind heroine who regains her

Popular appeal
(right) One of Collins' greatest gifts was to understand his audience and appeal to their interests – a talent he shared with his mentor, Charles Dickens. Both men had a penchant for popular melodrama based on domestic tragedy – recurrent themes included threats to the home and to the sanctity of family life. It was a rich vein to tap, and was echoed by the style of Victorian 'narrative painting' practised by, among others, their artist friend Augustus Egg. His series of three pictures entitled 'Past and Present' explored the results of a 'fall from grace' – Collins and Dickens were able to flesh out similar moral fables with their strong and endearing characters, dramatic plots and control of suspense and action.

The Frozen Deep
(below) Arctic voyage was the subject of a close collaboration between Collins and Dickens. They jointly wrote it, and both performed in the play to packed houses.

Arts Library, City of Manchester

BBC Hulton Picture Library

Maximum effect
Collins' financial success was immense. He developed the happy knack of making the most of his work, and frequently turned his tales into plays, and vice-versa until, like Dickens, he became a household name and a favourite subject for cartoons.

A. Egg 'Past & Present No.1' Tate Gallery

sight only to discover that her suitor (one of a pair of identical twins who both happen to be in love with her) has turned blue all over, to a legless poet called Miserimus Dexter.

One scathing review of what some eminent critics now consider to be his finest work, *The Moonstone,* concluded that 'We do not know of any books of which it is truer than of Mr Collins's to make the damaging remark, that nobody reads them twice, and that when the end of the first perusal is reached, everybody thinks his time has been wasted'. The fact that *The Moonstone* is still read and reread a century after the author's death is ample reply to the anonymous critic. There is no denying, however, that Wilkie Collins was what we would call today a 'popular' rather than a 'serious' novelist.

'KING PUBLIC'

He would not have minded the 'popular' tag any more than his friend and mentor Charles Dickens, who once summed up the purpose of writing as succinctly as it is possible to do so: 'You write to be read, of course.' For whatever the critics wrote, it was towards the ordinary audience, 'King Public' in Collins' phrase, that he and Dickens felt their primary obligation was to be directed.

Dickens' influence on Collins was incalculable. He encouraged him, employed him both as assistant editor and contributor on *Household Words* and *All the Year Round,* and even collaborated with him. The two authors were united in their regard for their readers' opinion, in their love of theatre (Collins dramatized his stories and novels, and both he and Dickens acted in them), and in their exub-

Bearing witness
Doubtless Collins' legal training predisposed him towards an interest in crime, criminals and detection. It also inspired the 'witness-in-the-box' narrative of his two major novels. Though his plots often seem improbable, many were based on real criminal cases he had witnessed, criminal records he had acquired in Paris, or from cases reported in Dickens' Household Words.

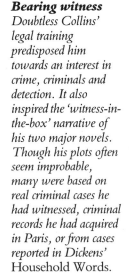

Mary Evans Picture Library

erant enjoyment of melodrama, suspense and storytelling. They also both possessed a prodigious amount of creative energy. In the three months prior to their European holiday in 1853, for example, while Dickens put the finishing touches to *Bleak House,* edited *Household Words* and dictated *A Child's History of England,* Collins wrote enough of his novel *Hide and Seek* to fill 600 printed pages.

A regular feature of the Dickens-Collins collaboration was their Christmas books. Sometimes they both wrote sections of the same story: 'Let us arrange to culminate in a wintry flight and pursuit across the Alps, under lonely circumstances, and against warnings. . .We shall get a very Avalanche of power out of it, and thunder it down on the readers' heads', Dickens wrote enthusiastically to Collins in 1867. He defied anyone to tell the difference between the sections that he had written and those written by Collins. No other author, it has been said, could have matched the great Dickens in style, liveliness and sheer storytelling skill. And only Collins could match his gusto.

INTERACTIVE READERS

Serial publication suited Collins as much as it did his older colleague. It was in monthly instalments in *All the Year Round* that *The Woman in White* first appeared in 1860. The method was eminently suitable for his mystery and detective fiction, tailor-made for increasing the suspense at the end of each episode. Issuing novels in serial form also made the most of the intimate relationship between novelist and reader. For the reader, it provided a greater sense of involvement with the novel and almost of participation with the novelist. This was not always completely illusory. For the serial writer could adapt the story according to public reaction.

Collins' sense of identification with his readers was remarkable. When they wrote to him, he answered at considerable length, offering detailed explanations of his writing methods. He went even further on one occasion, publishing his reply to a woman friend's question, 'How do you write your books?' In *How I Write My Books* he gives a blow-by-blow account of the process by which he created *The Woman in White*. He explains that he began with the central idea of 'a conspiracy to rob a woman of her identity', and goes on to describe how the idea itself suggested some of the chief characters: *A clever devil must conduct the conspiracy. Male devil or female devil? The sort of wickedness wanted seems to be a man's wickedness. Perhaps a foreign man. Count Fosco faintly shows himself to me before I know his name. I let him wait, and begin to think about the two women. They must be both innocent and both interesting. Lady Glyde dawns on me as one of the innocent victims. I try to discover the other – and fail. I try what a walk will do for me – and fail. I devote the evening to a new effort – and fail. Experience tells me to take no more trouble about it, and leave that other woman to come of her own accord. The next morning, before I have been awake more than ten minutes, my perverse brains set to work without consulting me. Poor Anne Catherick comes into my room and says, 'Try me.'*

Collins continues in a similar vein, pointing out that while he, the author, dictates the essential outline of the plot, it is the characters themselves who fill in the details. As the characters become fleshed out, so the plot develops and progresses.

Long arm of the Law
Collins' portraits of policemen lift his detective novels above the ordinary. He also brought the work of Scotland Yard (below) greater public attention.

Extraordinary as Collins' plots may seem, they are often based on real criminal cases. Maurice Méjans *Recueil des Causes Célèbres* (Records of Famous Trials), which was among a collection of criminal records that Collins bought while in Paris with Dickens, formed the basis of the plot for *The Woman in White*. And details in *The Moonstone* (such as the clue of a missing nightdress) can be traced to the detective work of the real-life policeman Inspector Whicher, on whom the character Sergeant Cuff is based. Collins' concern for authenticity went as far as having a murderous machine that featured in one of his stories manufactured – in order to ensure that the details he described were correct.

AUTHENTICITY

His factual detail may have originated in his legal training. And the process of the law not only influenced his themes and plots, it also inspired the 'witness-in-the-box' narrative method of his two major novels. The effectiveness of this technique occurred to him when he visited a criminal trial in 1856, and 'It came to me that a series of events in a novel would lend themselves well to an exposition like this. Certainly by the same means employed here, I thought, one could impart to the reader that acceptance, that sense of belief, which I saw produced here by the succession of testimonies so varied in form and nevertheless unified in their march towards the same goal.'

As in a real trial, the testimony of witnesses allows the 'evidence' in Collins' mysteries to build up little by little, sometimes confirming, sometimes confounding the reader's opinion of 'who-dunnit'. With each narrative, the tension and suspense increases until all the clues are revealed and the pieces fit together.

W.H. Hunt 'The Awakening Conscience'. Tate Gallery

R.G. Hutchinson 'Reading the Will'. Fine Art Photographic Library

Life after death

(above) In a Collins' novel, much of the action arises from the proceeds of a will, or from the lack of one. Women were – in his fiction and in fact – particularly vulnerable: they either lost their fortunes or became victim to unscrupulous gold-diggers.

Fallen women

(left) Holman Hunt's painting of 'The Awakening Conscience' was inspired by Dickens' Little Em'ly in David Copperfield. Collins also shared Dickens' sympathetic vision, and produced a long line of strongly drawn female characters that were as rich in detail and psychological authenticity as the woman in Holman Hunt's painting.

Character portraits

(right) Collins did not rely exclusively on complicated plots, mysterious events and dramatic action. Many of his fictional characters were fully fleshed-out and credible figures. Most unusual for his time and class were his portraits of women and servants.

For a writer of such a prolific nature, and with a career spanning over 40 years, it is surprising that Collins' work is limited to the years from 1860, when he published *The Woman in White,* to 1868 when he published *The Moonstone.* Between these years, he wrote *No Name* (1862) and the complex melodrama *Armadale* (1866). Only these four novels stand the test of time. In *No Name,* with its theme of illegitimacy and lost fortune, there is an indication of the social concerns that were to dominate (and most say, destroy) his later novels, causing the poet Swinburne to write: *What brought good Wilkie's genius nigh perdition? Some demon whispered – Wilkie! have a mission.*

For as Collins' distaste for the hypocrisy of Victorian society and its 'clap-trap morality' grew, so his attention focused on writing 'problem novels', a favourite theme being the fate of 'fallen women'. These 'problems' crystallized his skill, and testify that he had more humanity than his sensational books imply.

J. Finnie 'Maidservants'. Fine Art Photographic Library

WORKS·IN OUTLINE

Wilkie Collins was a prolific writer possessed by an energy and application only rivalled by his friend and collaborator, Charles Dickens. In the four decades from 1850 he published a staggering 25 novels, numerous short stories and 15 plays (several adapted from the novels).

Even his unlikely first novel – a classical romance set in the 5th century – enjoyed a reasonable success at the time, but Collins never returned to that outmoded genre. Instead he turned to the form that was to bring him immense fame and fortune: the melodramatic thriller.

Ironically, little of Collins' huge output has stood the test of time and public opinion. Twelve of his short stories have only recently been collected and republished together as *Tales of Terror and the Supernatural*, and only one play, *The Frozen Deep* (1857) still receives recognition. His claim to greatness rests on the four brilliant novels he wrote during the 1860s. *The Woman in White* (1860) is his spell-binding thriller of enduring appeal. *No Name* (1862) and *Armadale* (1866) are intricately constructed and eminently readable melodramas in similar vein. But *The Moonstone* (1868) is a truly splendid tale, brilliantly told – T.S. Eliot said it was 'the first, the longest, and the best of modern detective novels'. History has proved him right.

THE MOONSTONE
◆ 1868 ◆

Plucked from the head of an Indian moon-god shrine (right), the precious stone of the title is a fabulous diamond. In the course of the sacrilege, the thief kills the three Brahmins guarding it. Years later, the stone is bequeathed to Rachel Verinder on her 18th birthday. It disappears the same night. Who has stolen it, and how? The suspects include Rachel herself, her suitor Franklin Blake, Rosanna Spearman (a hunchbacked housemaid and ex-thief) and three sinister looking Indians claiming to be jugglers. Prototype police sleuth Sergeant Cuff (below) heads the investigation, but is thrown off the scent when Rosanna drowns herself. Only Rachel knows that her drug-induced suitor was the unwitting thief, and only the Indian 'jugglers' can exact revenge on the truly guilty party.

The Goddess Kali. Hindu miniature. Victoria & Albert Museum/Michael Holford

TALES OF TERROR AND THE SUPERNATURAL

A volume of Collins' short stories appeared in 1856 under the title *After Dark,* followed by a second volume – *The Queen of Hearts* – three years later. *Tales of Terror and the Supernatural* (1972) collect together the best from both volumes, and show the author to be a master of the macabre, of 'Tales of Suspense' and of the detection tale.

The Dream-Woman (below) is one of the best-known and most popular. It is a tale about unfortunate Isaac Scatchard, who lives uneventfully with his widowed mother until one night he has a horrific nightmare – a demented woman tries to murder him as he lies in bed. Years later, life catches up with the dream, and Isaac is reduced to a pathetic insomniac, snatching moments of sleep by day and on guard at night, certain that the Dream-Woman will strike again.

Collins' flair for mystery, suspense and melodrama was arguably better suited to the short story than to the full-length novel – this collection (published by Dover Publications in 1972) may well prove the point. The twelve very different stories make compulsive reading on a variety of intensely melodramatic themes.

BBC Hulton Picture Library

NO NAME

◆ 1862 ◆

Unhappy and happy marriages (left) are at the heart of this 'immoral book'. The spirited, illegitimate Magdalen Vanstone is driven to unscrupulous behaviour when her natural father – unhappily married to another woman – dies intestate. Magdalen and her illegitimate sisters are left penniless when the father's fortune goes to the nearest relative, Noel Vanstone, a sickly old fool. Magdalen sets out to get her hands on what she thinks, not unreasonably, is hers and her sisters' by natural right. With the aid of the scoundrel Captain Wragge, she snares the despised relative, who promptly dies. Outsmarted by his cunning housekeeper, Magdalen grows full of remorse at her own wickedness. She had won, then lost. In the end, she wins again – by marriage.

THE FROZEN DEEP

◆ 1857 ◆

Arctic exploration had seized the popular imagination and excited the two most popular writers of the day – Dickens and Collins. The friends responded, and collaborated on a 3-act melodramatic play on the subject; Dickens outlined the plot, Collins wrote the parts, both acted in it, but it was not published until 1874.

Unknown to each other, two suitors to the beautiful Clara Burnham are members of a doomed Arctic expedition: Richard Wardour (played by Dickens) is the rejected lover intent on revenge; Frank Aldersley (played by Collins) is the chosen suitor. Only when they are thrown together on a relief team do they become aware of their rivalry. In the event, Wardour sacrifices his own life to save Aldersley's and secure Clara's happiness. The collaboration led to yet more creativity – from it, Dickens conceived the character of the self-sacrificing, rejected lover who became Sydney Carton in *A Tale of Two Cities*.

ARMADALE

◆ 1866 ◆

Two Alan Armadales (right) make for a complicated but ingenious plot, full of intricate and inter-related strategies and coincidences. The story has a beautiful woman as its main character – Lydia Gwilt is a 35-year old flaming redhead whose ravishing features belie a lurid past. Forgery, bigamy, theft, murder, attempted suicide and a jail sentence are only some of her many misdemeanours. In the course of the novel, she attempts to add to this catalogue of crimes by first entrapping wealthy young Alan Armadale in marriage – for she is a gold-digger, too. When her plan is foiled, she attempts to murder him. Complexity piles on to complexity, and Lydia eventually marries the other Alan Armadale – a character very unlike his namesake. Longer and more complicated than his other novels, Collins controls the complicated plot to sustain the action and the suspense from one chapter to the next. His skill in so doing is all the more remarkable for the fact that the 'secret' of the plot is disclosed at an early stage. Lydia Gwilt is one of his most strongly drawn female characters, but the novel suffers from over-reliance on the power of coincidence.

Fear of the Madhouse

The image of the asylum in *The Woman in White* found an audience embarrassed by the phenomenon of madness. Conflicting interests all too often concealed a wretchedly inhumane treatment of the insane.

At the time when Wilkie Collins wrote *The Woman in White,* the mentally ill were feared and shunned by respectable society. The relatives of the insane tended to be ashamed of them, and most 'normal' people were glad to see lunatics put out of the way in special institutions.

Yet madhouses, and the 'mad doctors' associated with them, had a distinctly sinister reputation. In the public mind, an asylum was a place where, for questionable reasons, a person was shut up against her or his will, neglected and mistreated by brutal keepers, and often kept in confinement long after 'sanity' had been restored.

The unsavoury reputation of madhouses was based on a long history of real scandals and abuses, and although many reforms had been introduced by the mid-19th century, shocking facts about the treatment of the insane still came to light. In 1858, the year before Collins began work on *The Woman in White,* patients at two private madhouses were declared sane after an investigation. And one of them, a Mrs Turner, charged that the proprietor, as well as improperly detaining her, had sexually assaulted her.

Although Collins nowhere implies that there is anything amiss with the "prettily laid out" madhouse in *The Woman in White,* where Anne Catherick and Laura, Lady Glyde, are incarcerated, the horrors associated with such places certainly reinforced its emotional impact on Victorian readers.

Earlier attitudes to mental affliction were more open. Idiots and lunatics, although liable to be mocked and provoked, were tolerated within the community, and the 'village idiot' was a familiar figure. The tendency to segregate mad people by putting them in institutions became marked in the 18th century, but the notion that lunacy was a comic phenomenon lingered on.

The oldest public hospital specializing in the treatment of insanity was London's Bethlehem Hospital, whose origins dated back to the 14th century. Its name was soon contracted to Bethlem, which became in familiar speech the notorious 'Bedlam'. Here the unfortunate pauper inmates were put on show for the benefit of spectators who paid twopence a head to watch them, while hucksters sold fruit and nuts, and obliging keepers brought in beer for a small consideration. Public feeling changed slowly, and it was only in 1770 that the first restrictions were placed on visitors to Bedlam. But the hospital's infamous image – influencing attitudes to its inmates – continued well into the 19th century, and was reflected in popular ballads.

A social inconvenience
(right) Polite and well-regulated Victorian society was unable to understand, much less accept, the distressed and distressing behaviour of the insane. The lunatic was essentially an object of shame and fear, and was dealt with in true Victorian fashion by being 'put away' in institutions where their torments were neither seen nor heard.

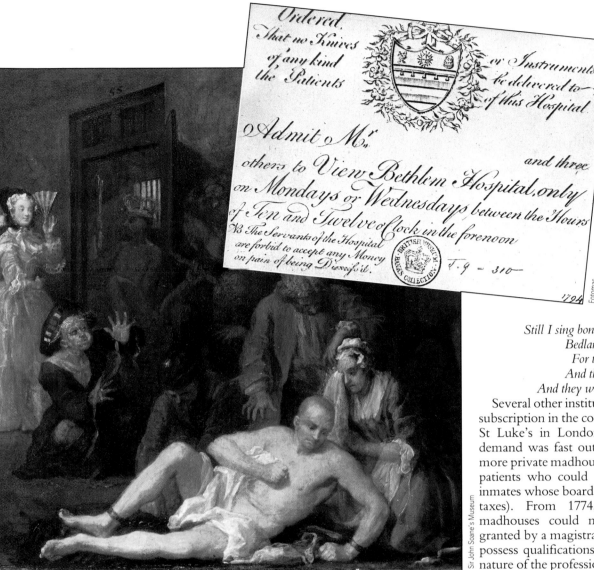

Fotomas

**Madhouse
entertainment**
*(left and inset) The first
lunatic asylum in England
was the notorious Bethlehem
or 'Bedlam' hospital. Here
inmates not only suffered
brutal ill-treatment, but,
until long into the 18th
century, were put on show
for the amusement of
fashionable ladies and
gentlemen and for the profit
of the proprietors.*

> *Still I sing bonnie boys, bonnie mad boys,*
> *Bedlam boys are bonnie.*
> *For they all go there,*
> *And they live on the air,*
> *And they want no drink nor money.*

Several other institutions were established by public
subscription in the course of the 18th century, notably
St Luke's in London and the York Asylum. But
demand was fast outrunning supply, and more and
more private madhouses were opened, catering to rich
patients who could afford to pay fees, and pauper
inmates whose board was funded from the rates (local
taxes). From 1774, the proprietors of private
madhouses could not operate without a licence
granted by a magistrate, but they were not obliged to
possess qualifications of any kind. Given the bizarre
nature of the professional treatment usually meted out
to mental patients, this was not necessarily a drawback.

DOUBLE STANDARDS

Public and private institutions varied greatly, and there
were compassionate and professional figures associated
with both. But if the public asylums were too often
neglectful and brutal, the private madhouse proprietor
– whose sole intention was to make a profit – faced a
double temptation: to spend as little time and money as
could be on poor patients, and to keep rich ones inter-
red, regardless of their actual mental state. As in so
many other matters, rich and poor people in the 19th
century were treated quite differently in the madhouse.

Since paupers were a charge on the rates, local
authorities tried to maintain them as cheaply as possible. But apart from Bethlem and a few other urban
institutions, there were no public places available for
Britain's poor who were mentally ill. Poor people who
became ill in any way usually ended up dependent on
charity and were simply placed in the workhouse,
alongside the old, infirm and unemployed.

Some were, however, boarded out with local people
who were prepared to take them in for a small pay-
ment. In these circumstances, the care of the insane was
rudimentary, and treatment was non-existent. Even in
Collins' day, when legislation had outlawed the practice, dangerous and violent lunatics were still sometimes kept in workhouses on the orders of negligent or
penny-pinching magistrates.

The mad wife
*(right) Mr Rochester's
tragically demented wife in*
Jane Eyre *was more than
just a character of fiction.
Charlotte Brontë herself
knew of instances where a
mad woman was looked
after at home by her family,
rather than be placed in an
institution. But she did not
know that the novelist
Thackeray, to whom she
dedicated the second edition
of* Jane Eyre, *himself had an
insane wife who was kept in
care. Like other
compassionate individuals at
the time, he was concerned
that his wife should have the
kindness and attention she
needed – and that an
institution for the treatment
of the insane would not
provide it.*

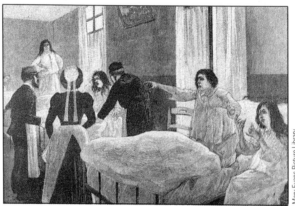

From the late 18th century, private madhouses were increasingly used as dumping grounds for pauper lunatics, and in some areas there was furious competition between rival houses for the custom of local authorities. The 'price-cutting wars' that ensued meant favourable terms for the authorities, but were rather less advantageous for the paupers. With only a few shillings a week to spend on each pauper inmate, the proprietors inevitably employed poorly paid, brutal keepers, and crowded their patients into filthy, unventilated sheds and outhouses, where they were chained up if they caused any trouble.

Such abuses most often came to light when a lunatic escaped or was removed from 'care', such as the inmate taken from Gate Helmsley in Yorkshire in 1847, who was dying 'in a filthy condition and with running wounds'. Official indifference was underlined by the 'improved' legislation, which until 1828 specifically excluded parish paupers from regulations about commitments and the inspection of premises.

APPALLING CONDITIONS

In terms of care and conditions, the poor got the worst of things in both private and public institutions. At York Asylum, despite its public character, rich patients were accepted and the pauper inmates were appallingly housed and neglected – so much so that, when an investigation began in 1815, an 'accidental' fire was started to burn down some of the most suspect buildings, and members of the staff destroyed incriminating records.

The polite term 'mechanical restraint' was used to describe the most economical method of controlling patients who were violent or simply obstreperous or restless. In reality, the term meant chains, manacles and a virtual Chamber of Horrors of contraptions which were found by 19th century investigators.

One of them, Edward Wakefield, created a sensation by his description of the conditions in which James Norris had been confined at Bethlem for 14 years. He had 'a stout iron ring. . .riveted round his neck' and chained to an iron bar on the wall. His arms were pinioned, his right leg was chained to the trough in which he slept, and additional chains, only twelve

Home and abroad
(above and top) In England, the many forms of madness and the complexity of its causes went virtually unrecognized; and treatment made no attempt to study the individual's case and domestic circumstances (top). Contemporary French doctors were, however, relatively enlightened, and the most famous founded asylums where their methods were put into practice. One of the most celebrated was Jeanne Esquirol's Maison de Santé *(above), where Thackeray's wife was a short-term patient. Thackeray was disturbed by the sight of 'wild fierce women rambling about in the garden' but considered it 'the very best place' in terms of compassionate treatment of the insane.*

inches long, made it impossible for him to do much more than either stand or lie down in one position, on his back.

Class, much more than sex, determined attitudes to the mentally disturbed, and dictated the treatment that was received. To the 'mad doctor', the rich were a different species from the poor. The Physician to Bethlem, Dr Thomas Monro, declared before a public enquiry that chains were 'fit only for the pauper lunatics: if a gentleman was put in irons he would not like it. I am not accustomed to gentlemen in irons; I never saw anything of the kind; it is a thing so totally abhorrent to my feelings that I never considered it necessary to put a gentleman in irons.'

He might have added that gentlemen and women (or their relations) could afford to pay for kindly individual attention, and were more likely to be listened to if they complained of being neglected or ill-treated. And if their families were compassionate, they had more chance of being looked after by a keeper than of being placed in an institution.

Some relatives might be the reverse of caring, however. In the 18th century it was not unknown for men and women to be put away because they were an embarrassment, had fallen in love with someone 'unsuitable', or were just in the way. As early as 1728, Daniel Defoe, the author of *Robinson Crusoe*, complained of 'the vile Practice so much in vogue among

Sir Luke Fildes 'Awaiting Admission to the Casual Ward', Royal Holloway College, University of London, Egham, Surrey/Bridgeman Art Library

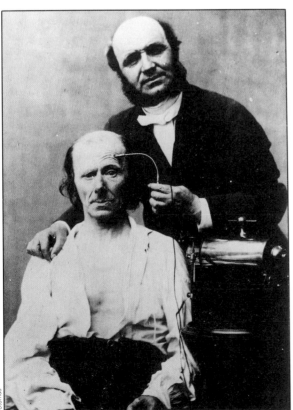

Fotomas

The plight of the poor
(above) The poor who became mentally ill were treated in the same way as those who were homeless, destitute, unemployed or physically sick. They were placed in the workhouse, where their illness, aggravated if not partly engendered by deprivation, received no attention at all.

The 'victim patient'
(left) Mental patients were acutely vulnerable to vicious medical practices, as the activities of the French doctor, M.G.B. Duchenne reveal. This photograph, taken in 1862, shows him with a patient he has electrocuted to achieve what he called 'electro-physiognomy'. This perverse practice he termed an 'art form'.

the better Sort. . .namely, the sending their wives to Mad-Houses at every Whim or Dislike, that they may be more secure and undisturb'd in their Debaucheries.'

Another motive was to secure an inheritance or to gain control of an estate, as in *The Woman in White*. Collins' story was based on a French case some 50 years earlier, and by Victorian times such schemes could only be executed through the ingenuity of a Count Fosco. Even so, an eminent medical man, John Conolly, warned in 1830, 'Let no one imagine that even now it is impossible or difficult to effect the seclusion of an eccentric man; or easy for him, when once confined, to regain his liberty.'

PROFITABLE CONFINEMENT

It was particularly difficult for gentlefolk to be released once confined in a private madhouse, for a wealthy patient's recovery threatened the place's profits. John Perceval, the son of the Prime Minister, Spencer Perceval, wrote two indignant volumes about his own incarceration during the early 1830s. 'I had to fight my way for two years,' he complains, 'wringing from my friends a gradual but tardy assent to the most urgent expostulations; not from the physicians. . .their maxim [is] to clutch and hold fast.'

Perceval was embittered by his family's attitude. They had put him away against his will, and thereafter abided by the self-interested opinions of 'experts', who were even allowed to oversee his letters to his mother.

And the shame attached to insanity was such that Perceval's relations regarded it as proof of his unsound mind that he wished to make public his past history by prosecuting the madhouse proprietors for their treatment of him.

Among Perceval's many grievances was the fact that no attempt was made to reason with him or explain what was being done. As a member of the upper class, he was outraged by the violation of his 'English liberties' and 'insulted and injured by the enforced use of the shower-bath and cold bath'. As far as medical treatment was concerned, pauper patients might well have felt thankful for neglect – for normal medical practice was little short of barbaric.

ALTERNATIVE REMEDIES

A gentleman may not have been manacled, but he was certainly bled, blistered, purged, dosed with bark, forced to vomit and plunged into hot and cold baths by responsible and attentive physicians. Much the same regime was imposed on King George III, whose protracted fits of madness between 1789 and his death in 1820 helped to make the subject an urgent public issue. Within a few decades, mainly due to men such as John Conolly, treatments were gradually becoming more humane and committed to understanding and coping with the patient's malady.

The new attitudes were backed up by changes in the law. From 1774, no person could be committed without a certificate signed by an apothecary, surgeon or physician, and proprietors of private madhouses needed to obtain a licence and submit to regular (if not very effective) inspection. Further progress was slow because so many vested interests were involved in private madhouses. It was not only the proprietors and physicians who resisted change, but the House of Lords also tended to defend the interests of the investors above those of the inmates.

Only in 1845 were magistrates compelled to set up county asylums, which at last removed paupers from private madhouses. In the same year, a Board of Commissioners in Lunacy was established, with powers to inspect all public and private asylums, and to monitor the situation of all patients under restraint. Certification of insanity was also tightened up, although it was not until 1890 that a magistrate's order was required before a patient could be committed against his or her will.

The new system of public asylums had defects of its own. But the reform movement represented a significant advance in care and humanity in the treatment of the insane, which helped to combat those fearful images evoked for Victorian readers by the madhouse in *The Woman in White*.

Both ends of the scale
The case of James Norris (above left) typified the inhuman methods used to 'restrain' pauper patients. An inmate of the Bethlem Hospital, he was manacled and chained by the neck and limbs, making him unable to sit or lie in comfort. Although such indignities were not inflicted on well-born patients – like George III (above) – they too might undergo the painful and gruelling treatments which were automatically meted out, whatever the illness. George III, a victim of porphyria, was insane for the last 30 years of his life, and his condition contributed to an awakening of public concern about the problem of insanity.

ARTHUR CONAN DOYLE

⟵ *1859 - 1930* ⟶

The runaway success of his brain–child Sherlock Holmes propelled
Conan Doyle from obscurity as an impoverished doctor into the
limelight of public approval. Yet the character was to prove a bane as
well as a blessing, and to conflict endlessly with Conan Doyle's
self–image as a 'serious' historical novelist. Tireless and outspoken in
pursuing his interests – which ranged from patriotism to spiritualism
– Conan Doyle was, until his death, one of the most celebrated
figures of the Victorian age.

'Steel True, Blade Straight'

Like his fictional heroes, Conan Doyle was a man of action and honour, his personal exploits bringing him as much fame in his lifetime as did his literary creations.

One of the most eminent of all Victorians, Sir Arthur Conan Doyle is known today almost exclusively as the creator of Sherlock Holmes. But in his own day, Conan Doyle was a most celebrated public figure. On the eve of the Boer War, when he called on young men of Britain to support Queen and country he described himself in a letter to his mother as 'the most famous man in England'.

Arthur Conan Doyle was born in Edinburgh on 22 May 1859, the second child of Mary Foley and Charles Doyle. His mother came from a distinguished Scottish military family, and his father was an alcoholic draughtsman. Mary Foley, known as 'The Ma'am', was a formidable personality who had a strong influence over her children. Conan Doyle later described her 'sweet face, her sensitive mouth, her peering, short-sighted eyes, her general suggestion of a plump little hen, who is still on the alert about her chickens.' She brought up her seven children with a strict code of honour and, despite the family's poverty, imbued them with immense pride in their ancestry. Conan Doyle was to turn to her for advice throughout his life.

RIGOROUS SCHOOLING

The Ma'am was determined that he should have a good education and, since the Doyles were a devout Catholic family, sent her son to Stonyhurst, a Jesuit public (private) school in Lancashire. The comforts of home were suddenly replaced by a dour, demanding lifestyle fed by a daily diet of prayers, lessons, stews and sport. Conan Doyle found solace in fiction and became a fervent admirer of Sir Walter Scott, and of Edgar Allan Poe's *The Murders in the Rue Morgue*.

On leaving Stonyhurst, Arthur spent a year at a Jesuit school in Austria before deciding to become a doctor. On the Ma'am's advice he studied medicine at

Edinburgh University, graduating when he was 22. Meanwhile, the young student paid his way by working as a clerk for Dr Joseph Bell, a surgeon who later became the model for Sherlock Holmes.

Bell had some of the hallmarks of the great fictional detective, delighting in impressing his students with clever deductions about patients, based on close observation of their clothes, mannerisms and behaviour.

Conan Doyle was still a student when his father, Charles Doyle, was admitted into a nursing home, leav-

Stanley Mackenzie Collection

The Ma'am

(below left) Conan Doyle remained close to his mother – affectionately known as 'The Ma'am' – until her death. He later recalled her gift for story-telling, and how her voice would sink 'to a horror-stricken whisper when she came to a crisis in her narrative'. He maintained that he was indebted to her for his early love of literature.

Father's fantasies

Epileptic and alcoholic, Conan Doyle's father became increasingly immersed in his own fantasy world – as his self-portrait below suggests – and he finally had to be cared for in a series of homes.

Scottish youth

(right) Edinburgh was the scene of Conan Doyle's early childhood and his days as a medical student. He lived at home to save money, and spent five gruelling years studying subjects which often, he felt, had only 'a very indirect bearing on the art of curing'.

Fine Art Society/Bridgeman Art Library

Victoria and Albert Museum/Bridgeman Art Library

Jean-Loup Charmet

ing the family in difficult financial straits. The following year the young medic began providing for his mother by taking a job as ship's surgeon on the *Hope*, a 400-ton whaler bound for the Arctic. On the seven-month voyage he experienced a completely new world, witnessing the slaughter of Greenland seals, harpooning a whale and nearly drowning in the icy waters. He also made some much-needed money, returning to Edinburgh with 50 gold sovereigns for his mother, and enough to see him through the last year of his course.

DOCTOR AT SEA

The following winter Conan Doyle made a journey of a very different kind aboard the *SS Mayumba*, a cargo and passenger ship bound for West Africa. There was none of the exhilaration of his last voyage, only a sequence of near disasters. Gales in the Bay of Biscay nearly sank the ship; blackwater fever and malaria attacked passengers and crew; Conan Doyle nearly died from typhoid; and on the journey home the ship caught fire – the hull was still smoking when the *Mayumba* docked at Liverpool in January 1882.

That year, a telegram arrived from Plymouth: 'STARTED HERE LAST JUNE. COLOSSAL SUCCESS. COME DOWN BY NEXT TRAIN IF POSSIBLE. PLENTY OF ROOM FOR YOU. SPLENDID OPENING.' It had been sent by an old student friend named George Budd, an energetic if unscrupulous young doctor with countless wild ideas for making a fortune. Conan Doyle joined his friend, but although Budd's new Plymouth practice was indeed crowded with patients, few had any money – and under pressure from his Ma'am, Conan Doyle ended the partnership, wrenching the brass nameplate from the door with his bare hands.

Ship's surgeon

(above) With his father no longer able to keep the family, Conan Doyle, like his sisters, took on the role of family provider. While still a third-year student, he signed up as ship's surgeon on a whaler. The voyage through the ice-packed seas of the Arctic gave him a taste of adventure – and earned him £50 which he later passed on to the Ma'am.

Amusing quackery

(right) Conan Doyle imagined that due application would lead directly to an 'honorary surgeonship'. In the event, the newly-fledged graduate joined the practice of a gifted quack, George Budd. The job was entertaining but far from lucrative, and Conan Doyle was soon supplementing his income by his pen.

F. Holl: Doubtful Hope (Detail) Forbes Magazine Collection/Bridgeman Art Library

But Conan Doyle did not return to Edinburgh. Instead, he set up on his own in Southsea, a suburb of Portsmouth, where he was joined by his nine-year-old brother Innes. The boy wrote cheerfully to the Ma'am telling her how 'we have made three bob this week. We have vaxeinated a baby and got hold of a man with consumtion[sic].' But business was very quiet. Had it not been for two crucial developments, it is very unlikely that Conan Doyle would have stayed in Southsea for the next nine years.

The first was his marriage, in August 1885, to Louise Hawkins, the sister of one of his patients. The second was the invention of his master detective Sherlock Holmes. To pass the time and make some money, Arthur had begun writing stories for publication. His notebook records the emergence of his future fictional heroes: 'Ormond Sacker – from Afghanistan. Lived at 221b Upper Baker Street. Sherrinford Holmes – the Laws of Evidence. Reserved, sleepy-eyed young man – philosopher – collector of rare Violins.' By the end of their first adventure, Sacker had become Dr John Watson and Sherrinford had evolved into Sherlock, the two heroes of *A Study in Scarlet*.

MAKING A NAME

The story was published in *Beeton's Christmas Annuals* in December 1887, earning its author a welcome, if paltry £25. But since Conan Doyle's ambition was to write historical novels, not detective thrillers, he had started *Micah Clarke*, a romance about the 17th-century Monmouth rebellion. When this was first published in 1889, it was an instant success and encouraged him to embark on a medieval tale entitled *The White Company*. Holmes, however, had not been forgotten. *A Study in Scarlet* had slowly been gaining admirers, and a new novel, *The Sign of Four*, was commissioned by an American publisher.

Conan Doyle, now the father of a baby daughter named Mary Louise, had at last earned enough from his writings to escape from the provincial life of Southsea. In 1890, he travelled to Berlin to observe the experiments of a Dr Robert Koch, who had announced a possible cure for tuberculosis. The following year he went – with Louise – to Vienna to study ophthalmics for six months. When they returned to England, they moved to London, and Conan Doyle opened a consulting room in Devonshire Place.

First marriage
(above left) Conan Doyle married Louise Hawkins in 1885, when he was a struggling young doctor. But their happiness was to be shattered eight years later, when Louise was diagnosed as having consumption. Believing that country air might help, Conan Doyle built her a large house in Surrey, where he looked after her devotedly until her death.

Interval in Vienna
(above) In search of a speciality, Conan Doyle went to Vienna with Louise, to study eye medicine. But he soon abandoned the lectures because he could not follow them, and wrote a short book instead.

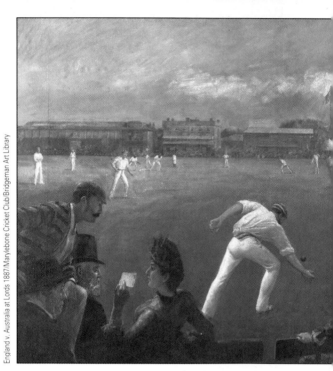

Fact or Fiction

THE REAL SHERLOCK HOLMES

Conan Doyle modelled his famous detective on Dr Joseph Bell, a surgeon and criminal psychologist who lectured at the Edinburgh Infirmary. Bell had the domed forehead, acquiline nose and cool manner that distinguished Holmes, and like him showed remarkable powers of deduction based on close observation.

He deduced, for example, that the bare patch on one patient's corduroy trousers indicated his trade as a cobbler, the patch being worn by constant friction as he hammered shoes. His 'diagnosis' was perfectly correct.

Sporting man of letters
(below) Until well into middle age, Conan Doyle took a vigorous delight in sport of all kinds. Cricket was his great passion – he played for the MCC (Marylebone Cricket Club) and scored a century on his first visit to Lord's cricket ground. He even faced the legendary W. G. Grace, bowling him out on one memorable occasion.

The venture, however, was a complete flop – in six months not a single patient climbed his stairs. So, instead of practising medicine, Conan Doyle started writing full-time in the surgery and, in 1891, published six Sherlock Holmes stories in the new and immensely popular *Strand Magazine*. Ironically, he still regarded the Holmes stories as a distraction from his real vocation as a historical novelist, and resented the amount of time he spent composing them. But they provided an invaluable income, and the editor commissioned a further six stories at £50 a piece.

With the *Strand Magazine's* circulation passing half a million, Conan Doyle's fortunes were transformed. He moved his family to a house in South Norwood and negotiated a cool £1,000 for the 1892 Holmes series. He started mixing in literary circles, and befriended Jerome

K. Jerome, author of *Three Men in a Boat*, and J.M. Barrie, the future author of *Peter Pan*. Yet he was still reluctant to tie himself to Holmes, and he and the Ma'am discussed his plans for killing off the detective.

In November 1892, Louise gave birth to a son, Alleyne Kingsley, but there were signs that her health was deteriorating. A journey to Switzerland, with a visit to the spectacular Reichenbach Falls, did nothing to cure her and, when they returned to London, she was diagnosed as suffering from consumption. At the same time Conan Doyle finally decided that he had to put an end to the Holmes saga, dispatching the great detective over the Reichenbach Falls, locked in a fatal struggle with the arch criminal Moriarty in *The Final Problem*. But when the story appeared in December 1893, his readers bombarded the magazine with letters of grief and outrage. Conan Doyle escaped most of the furore. After his father's death in October, he spent a holiday in Switzerland where he sought to relieve his depression by skiing, tobogganing and climbing.

DIVERSE INTERESTS

Since Conan Doyle had by now resolved his financial problems he was free, when he returned to England, to pursue his wide-ranging interests. He was an enthusiastic and capable sportsman – he played cricket and soccer for Portsmouth – and turned out for the MCC on a number of occasions, scoring on his first appearance at Lord's Cricket Ground. He also pursued his interest in psychic phenomena, joining the British Society for Psychical Research. And in 1895, he had a house built in Surrey, so that Louise could escape London's fumes.

At this point Conan Doyle turned to writing drama. His stage play *Waterloo* was a great success in London – so too was a series of comic tales about a dashing Napoleonic cavalry officer entitled *The Exploits of Brigadier Gerard*. But the smooth pattern of the novelist's life was transformed when, in March 1897, he fell in love with Jean Leckie, a young Scotswoman who lived with her parents in Blackheath. She returned his devotion, but he insisted that they should resist the temptation of physical affection while Louise lived. And they both lived by that decision, which committed them to ten years of exhausting self-denial. As usual, Arthur told the Ma'am, but Louise never found out about the 'other woman'.

Conan Doyle reached the age of 40 healthy, wealthy and deeply frustrated. Meanwhile Louise had become a severe invalid, her body wasted by tuberculosis, while arthritis wracked the joints of both hands. Conan Doyle filled his time writing stage plays and stories, riding to hounds, ballooning and holding clay pigeon shoots in the grounds of his house. In 1899, however, the declaration of war against the Boers channelled his energy in another direction. He travelled to the barracks to volunteer in person, only to be rejected as overweight. The following year, however, he was accepted and was sent to South Africa as a senior physician with a private field hospital.

Conan Doyle's war experience transformed him from a celebrity to a pillar of the Establishment. Although he completed only three months of field duty at Bloemfontein, the conditions he saw there – with up to 60 patients a day dying of typhoid – affected him

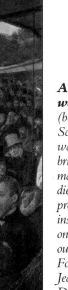

A long-awaited wedding
(below) A young Scotswoman, Jean Leckie, was Conan Doyle's second bride. The couple were married the year after Louise died, having met ten years previously. They had fallen instantly in love, but agreed on a 'platonic' relationship out of loyalty to Louise. Fourteen years his junior, Jean was to bear Conan Doyle two sons and a daughter.

deeply. When he returned to Britain, he found that General Kitchener and the army were under attack for their conduct of the war, and was so incensed that he defended them with a 50,000-word pamphlet on *The War in South Africa*. More than a million copies were sold in Britain. Two years later Conan Doyle was rewarded by a grateful King Edward VII, who knighted him at Buckingham Palace, creating him Deputy Lieutenant of Surrey.

The following year, 1903, saw the revival of Sherlock Holmes. *McClure's Magazine* in New York offered Conan Doyle the then fabulous sum of $5,000 for just six stories, and insisted that Holmes must emerge from the churning foam of Reichenbach, alive and dripping. Conan Doyle duly obliged, and his hero returned in *The Empty House* after a lengthy journey around the world.

Three years later, in July 1906, Louise died after 13 years of illness, and was buried in Surrey. Conan Doyle was too disturbed by her death to continue writing, but, later that year, immersed himself in a real-life detective case. An Indian solicitor named George Edalji had been imprisoned in 1903 for the brutal killing of a horse. He denied any involvement. Alerted to the peculiarities of the case, Conan Doyle studied every scrap of information he could find. Within months he had proved that Edalji had been convicted on grossly flawed evidence and revealed the true identity of the assailant. Edalji was released in 1907.

On 18th September that year, Conan Doyle married Jean Leckie and the two set off for a honeymoon cruise through the eastern Mediterranean, visiting Greece, Egypt and Turkey. On their return they moved into a large new house at Windlesham in Sussex.

Despite his support for the British Empire, Conan Doyle was not uncritical of the Establishment. Though he had stood for Parliament as a Liberal Unionist candidate for Edinburgh, and later for Hardwick, he was ready to oppose injustice wherever he saw it. In 1909 he wrote a pamphlet entitled *The Crime of the Congo*, to expose the cruelties perpetrated on Africans by Belgian colonists. And the following year he devoted himself to the cause of a German Jew named Oscar Slater, who had been falsely convicted of murder.

On this occasion Conan Doyle could achieve no dramatic breakthrough as in the Edalji affair. The legal authorities turned a blind eye to a long campaign conducted through the newspapers, in which Conan Doyle demonstrated that Slater, though an acknowledged pimp and petty criminal, was innocent. The wronged man spent 18 years in jail before being released, suddenly, with no pardon or compensation.

Conan Doyle's campaign urging Britain to prepare for war with Germany, and warning of the U-boat threat, was more effective. His efforts won him the support of the young Winston Churchill. When war did break out, he wrote a pamphlet *To Arms* urging volunteers to enlist, and set up his own local platoon.

At the front
(below) Conan Doyle's patriotism was fired by the outbreak of the Boer War. Although already 40, he wanted to enlist as an example to the 'young athletic sporting men' of England. He joined a hospital unit which followed the advance of General Roberts on Pretoria. The team had to cope with a devastating typhoid outbreak, but Conan Doyle took the opportunity to talk to Boer prisoners, and participants in the British campaign, not least Roberts himself. Later he wrote up his impressions in The Great Boer War.

THE SPIRIT WORLD

Increasingly convinced of physical existence after death, Conan Doyle came to believe that the soul was 'a complete duplicate of the body'. He announced his conversion to spiritualism in 1916, and thereafter channelled his new-found zeal into books, articles and lectures, spending £250,000 on promoting the cause. His enthusiasm even led him to declare a belief in fairies.

The fey and the fake
(left) Photographs of tiny winged female forms, produced by two Yorkshire girls, sparked off Conan Doyle's unflinching belief in fairies. To him they were as 'real' as they appear in this illustration by his uncle (above). The photographs were denounced as fakes, but Conan Doyle, unshakeable in his conviction, went on to state it openly in The Coming of the Fairies. *The ridicule this brought down on his head left Conan Doyle quite unperturbed.*

John Cutten Associates

British Library/Bridgeman Art Library

Jean-Loup Charmet

In defence of a traitor
*Sir Roger Casement (right),
an Irish nationalist who had
supported Germany from
the outset of World War
One, was, in 1916, under
sentence of execution as a
traitor. Conan Doyle had
been impressed by
Casement's exposure of
imperialist atrocities in the
Belgian Congo, and believed
that his recent pro-German
activities were proof that the
man was mentally
unbalanced. Conan Doyle
campaigned energetically for
a reprieve right up to the last
moment, inspired by the
injustice of the sentence – but
did not succeed.*

Mansell Collection

In 1916 he visited British forces in France and Italy, and like many of his generation, was shattered by the realities of war. In the course of it, he lost his son Kingsley and his brother Innes, as well as several close friends. He was also deeply saddened by the execution of Sir Roger Casement, an Irish nationalist convicted of treasonous conspiracy with the Germans. Conan Doyle was steadfast in his defence of Casement despite the smear campaign against the prisoner.

In the last decade of his life, Conan Doyle continued writing Holmes stories, but devoted his time increasingly to spiritualism. He went on lecture tours to America, Australia, Africa and Europe, spreading the gospel of psychic communications. After the Ma'am died in 1921, Jean became Conan Doyle's spirit medium, whereby he believed he could contact the dead members of his family. Astonishingly, in 1922, he even declared his belief in fairies after seeing some – presumably trick – photographs of two dancing fairies.

For his spiritualist activities he was ridiculed by the world's press, and his cause was not helped by the exposure of numerous fraudulent mediums. But his home life was tranquil and happy. Jean had borne him two sons and a daughter, and his old age was unmarred by ill-health or mental decay. He still enjoyed golf and long walks across the Weald, and he continued to write prolifically. But he also felt the need for greater privacy, and bought another house at Bignell Wood in the New Forest where he could escape the public gaze.

By 1929, however, his health had begun to decline. He was suffering regular heart pains, and was unable to speak on Armistice Day at the Albert Hall. Early in 1930, he was shocked by an internal dispute among colleagues in the Society for Psychical Research and resigned after 37 years of membership. Tired and anxious, he retreated to Windlesham, wrote his will, and tried to rest. The end was not far away. Early in the morning of 7th July 1930, Sir Arthur Conan Doyle died, sitting in his large basket chair, looking out across the garden. He was buried beside the summer-house, and his grave was marked by a simple oak slab on which were carved four words of epitaph: 'Steel True, Blade Straight.'

Spreading the word
*(below) In later life, Conan
Doyle devoted his time and
energy increasingly to
spiritualism. It influenced
both his fiction and his
non-fiction, and he travelled
widely giving lectures on the
subject. This photograph of
1923 shows the entire Doyle
family at Victoria Station,
en route for a lecture tour of
America.*

BBC Hulton Picture Library

THE ADVENTURES OF SHERLOCK HOLMES

Three stories selected from Sherlock Holmes' casebook illustrate the detective's legendary powers of deduction, as he unravels crimes which remain a mystery to his faithful biographer, Watson.

Sherlock Holmes and Dr John Watson make up one of the greatest double acts of literature. Their fans still think of them almost as real people. In 1987 – the centenary of Holmes' 'birth' in *A Study in Scarlet* – about 70 letters arrived each week at the Abbey National Building Society, 221B Baker Street, addressed to Mr Sherlock Holmes.

The dozen short stories narrated by Dr Watson in *The Adventures of Sherlock Holmes* contain the essence of the enduring Holmes-Watson magic. The action proceeds at a gallop, with a cast of characters from all walks of life. There is the beautiful opera singer and adventuress, Irene Adler, the one woman ever to cause Holmes to reconsider the disdain he feels for womankind. And her royal lover, the magnificent Wilhelm Gottsreich Sigismond von Ormstein, involves the detective in the intriguing *Scandal in Bohemia*. At the other end of the social scale, a red-haired pawnbroker paid four pounds a week for copying out the *Encyclopedia Britannica* by hand, plays a crucial role in the mystery posed by *The Redheaded League*.

A closer look at just three of the twelve stories in the collection will highlight the themes and merits which recur throughout the case-book. Human frailty and greed, treachery and honour – Conan Doyle's favourite themes – are in rich supply.

THE SPECKLED BAND

How can a murder be perpetrated upon a victim who is alone in a locked room? This most famous of Sherlock Holmes short stories is liberally strewn with red herrings as well as clues. The story is shot through with fear, made all the more intense by the decaying ancient mansion where the main action occurs.

Holmes and Watson, still bachelors, are

> *"'There is no mystery, my dear madam,' said he, smiling. 'The left arm of your jacket is spattered with mud in no less than seven places... There is no vehicle save a dog-cart which throws up mud in that way, and then only when you sit on the left-hand side of the driver.'"*

Family murder
(left) Helen Stoner's sinister stepfather follows her from their Surrey mansion to 221B Baker Street where she seeks the help of Sherlock Holmes (inset). Helen fears that her life is in danger, and though the identity of the would-be killer is obvious to detective and reader alike, the story has a sting in its tail.

Mistaken identity?
When Mrs St Clair (above) leaves the quiet respectability of her Kent home for a trip to London, the last thing she expects to see is her businessman husband disappearing from a dockside opium den (right). It appears that Neville St Clair's body has been dumped in the Thames. But appearances can be deceptive. . .

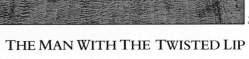

visited early one morning by a veiled woman dressed in black. Their breezy mood is soon dispelled when she raises her veil – " . . . we could see that she was indeed in a pitiable state of agitation, her face all drawn and grey, with restless, frightened eyes, like those of some hunted animal."

Helen Stoner lives with her stepfather, last of an ancient line, the Roylotts of Stoke Moran. They live in reduced circumstances on the money left by Helen's mother to her daughters. Their mother had died in a train crash, and Helen and her twin sister Julia had looked after the crumbling house where no servants would remain. Their stepfather, Dr Grimesby Roylott had, over the years, become an increasingly reclusive, violent man whose only friends were gypsies.

Two years before Helen's visit to 221B Baker Street, Julia – who was due to be married – died in mysterious circumstances. During a wild storm Helen heard her sister scream out in terror in the next bedroom, and ran into

the corridor as Julia's door swung open. Julia died in her sister's arms shrieking, *"O, my God! Helen! It was the band! The speckled band!"*

Helen herself is now engaged to be married and, to her horror, has started to hear the strange nightly whistling that preceded Julia's death. There is little doubt in anyone's mind that Dr Roylott killed Julia to forestall the loss of income which would result from her marriage, and is now likely to kill Helen for the same reason. These convictions are strengthened when Roylott bursts into Holmes' chambers and threatens him. The only question is: how does he intend to effect the murder?

Holmes and Watson make haste to visit the ancestral home and prevent the murder. They conceal themselves in "absolute darkness" in the fateful bedroom.
"Twelve o'clock, and one, and two, and three, and still we sat waiting silently for whatever might befall." . . .

THE MAN WITH THE TWISTED LIP

The contrast between the characters of Holmes and Watson is particularly marked in this story, which takes place after Watson's marriage, when he has a medical practice in Paddington. Holmes is now living more perilously than ever, and is first introduced disguised as an old opium addict in a dockside drug den.

One summer evening, Watson is visiting a sleazy opium den, the 'Bar of Gold', to rescue an addicted patient, when he happens upon

> "'I suppose, Watson,' said he, 'that you imagine that I have added opium-smoking to cocaine injections and all the other little weaknesses on which you have favoured me with your medical views.'"

Edimage: Inset: Fine Art Photographic Library

Holmes wearing his disturbingly real disguise.

"Through the gloom one could dimly catch a glimpse of bodies lying in strange fantastic poses, bowed shoulders, bent knees, heads thrown back and chins pointing upwards, with here and there a dark, lack-lustre eye turned upon the newcomer."

Holmes, in pursuit of investigations of his own, catches Watson's attention, and enlists his assistance. Soon they are trundling into the Kent countryside to the house of Holmes' client, a Mrs St Clair, whose husband Neville has disappeared.

Neville St Clair, a City businessman, left for London the previous Monday, as usual. Summoned by a telegram that same day to pick up a package at a shipping office, Mrs St Clair was astonished to catch sight of her husband disappearing backwards from an upper window, as if dragged – and this in the most unsavoury district of London's East End.

Running into the building – through the 'Bar of Gold' – she was prevented from going upstairs by the owner. By the time she returned with the police, her husband was nowhere to be found. The only occupant of the upper-floor room was a well-known local beggar, a hideous cripple called Hugh Boone. But behind a curtain were her husband's shoes, socks, hat and watch. On the bedroom window-sill overlooking the river, were spots of blood. The beggar was arrested, and at low tide, Neville St Clair's coat, weighted down with coins, was found in the mud.

But has a murder taken place? At the St Clair house the missing man's wife reveals a letter to Holmes, written hurriedly in her husband's hand: *"Dearest, do not be frightened. All will come well. There is a huge error which it may take some little time to rectify. Wait in patience. – Neville."*

In the Background

HOLMES' LONDON

Among the attractions of the Sherlock Holmes stories are the vivid images they provide of the bustling metropolis at the end of the last century: the sight and smell of the fogs that arose from a million coal fires; the ever-present sound of horses' hooves and the rattling wheels of the city's eleven thousand cabs and hansoms; the damp, cobbled streets, glistening from the rain; the dim gas-lighting. The scene is part of the Holmes magic.

Gas-lit streets
London's famous landmarks such as St Paul's Cathedral and Ludgate Circus are transformed by the eerie glow of the gas lights and the silhouettes of hansom cabs into the twilight world of Sherlock Holmes.

Holmes prepares himself to work the problem out in his idiosyncratic fashion, collecting pillows and cushions to construct *"a sort of Eastern divan, upon which he perched himself cross-legged, with an ounce of shag tobacco and a box of matches laid out in front of him."*

When Watson wakes at dawn, all the tobacco has gone and Holmes has solved the mystery. For Holmes' method is to pursue the logic of the facts until only one answer remains.

THE BLUE CARBUNCLE

There is a light-heartedness about this 'goose-chase' in keeping with its Christmas setting – it is the only time we meet Holmes and Watson at this season. When Watson visits Holmes on 27 December, he finds him studying a battered old hat, found by the commissionaire of 221B Baker Street. The commis-

Wild goose chase

A Christmas goose dropped in the street can solve the mystery of a jewel theft, but not before Holmes and Watson have traced its last movements through the pubs and markets of London (left). The man who dropped the bird also left his hat on the pavement, where it was picked up by the commissionaire of 221B Baker Street – who presented it to Holmes. When Watson pays a Christmas visit to Holmes (below), he finds him lounging in his rooms exercising his massive powers of deduction on the battered old hat. Only when the commissionaire discovers that the goose's crop contains a diamond does idle speculation turn to detective inquiry.

> *"'Remember, Watson, that though we have so homely a thing as a goose at one end of this chain, we have at the other a man who will certainly get seven years' penal servitude, unless we can establish his innocence.'"*

the goose's movements, back via the owner of the hat, to a public-house goose-club and on to a Covent Garden stall-holder and beyond. Their pursuit constitutes a guided tour of central London, on the cold, clear December night – "the breath of the passers-by blew out into smoke like so many pistol shots."

Someone else is also eager to trace the original goose. Knowing that this goose-chaser is likely to be the diamond thief, Holmes entices him to Baker Street. As befits a Christmas story, Holmes is happy to have solved the problem and to have saved an innocent man from jail. Since the blue carbuncle is recovered, he lets the thief go, in an expression of seasonal forgiveness.

"'After all, Watson,' said Holmes, reaching up his hand for his clay pipe, 'I am not retained by the police to supply their deficiencies.'" The reader is content, having been given an entertaining glimpse of a cross-section of London life from the Countess of Morcar's suite at the Hotel Cosmopolitan, to the gas-fires and marble slabs of Covent Garden market.

sionaire had interrupted a scuffle between a gang of roughs and a man carrying a Christmas goose. At his intervention, everyone – including the victim of the attack – fled, leaving the goose and the hat in the road. Holmes turns his powers of deduction on the hat in order to discover the owner. He comes to the conclusion that the man is a well-to-do intellectual, fallen on hard times, probably due to drink; that his wife has ceased to love him; and that he does not have gas laid on at his house.

When the goose's crop is found to contain a blue carbuncle diamond (instantly recognized by Holmes as belonging to the Countess of Morcar), what began as an idle exercise becomes a criminal investigation. A plumber is already under arrest for the theft of the stone, which has been missing for several days from the Countess's hotel room.

Thus begins a complex process of tracing

CHARACTERS IN FOCUS

Criminals and clients from every class of Victorian society people *The Adventures of Sherlock Holmes.* Each has his or her own, often very strange, story to tell, but many reflect fictional conventions. The wronged woman, the wicked stepfather, the master criminal and the grovelling small-time thief all make an appearance. But the stars of the stories are, of course, the dependable, conventional Dr John Watson, and his brilliantly unorthodox partner, Mr Sherlock Holmes.

WHO'S WHO

Sherlock Holmes   The first consulting detective. His life is dedicated to the art of logical deduction.

Dr John Watson   His loyal friend and chronicler.

THE SPECKLED BAND

Dr Grimesby Roylott   The violent master of the ancient Roylott home. A man with a mysterious past.

Helen Stoner   His step-daughter. A woman of thirty, who fears for her life.

THE MAN WITH THE TWISTED LIP

Neville St Clair   A City gent who goes missing, presumed dead. Last seen in an opium den.

Mrs St Clair   His wife. The last person to see him before his disappearance.

The Lascar   The sinister proprietor of the opium den. He has "sworn vengeance" on Holmes.

Hugh Boone   An ugly beggar who sleeps above the opium den.

THE BLUE CARBUNCLE

Peterson   The commissionaire at 221B Baker Street. He brings home a goose and hat that he finds after a street scuffle.

Henry Baker   The owner of the hat and the goose.

Mr Breckinridge   A Covent Garden stall-holder, who sold the goose to Baker. Unwilling to give information, he succumbs to a wager.

James Ryder   Head attendant at the Hotel Cosmopolitan, where the 'blue carbuncle' diamond was stolen.

Fine Art Photographic Library

Holmes' loyal side-kick, Dr John Watson has been invalided out of the army, and is a practising physician. The two men (below) became friends when they shared lodgings at 221B Baker Street. By the time he is chronicling *The Adventures*, Watson is happily married, but he is nevertheless prepared to break the law and even risk life and limb at his friend's bidding. His admiration for Holmes is immense: "I trust that I am not more dense than my neighbours, but I was always oppressed with a sense of my own stupidity in my dealings with Sherlock Holmes."

THE SPECKLED BAND

A lady dressed in black (above), in mourning for her sister and as frightened as "some hunted animal" seeks Holmes' help. She fears that, like her sister, she will die in mysterious circumstances before her intended wedding day. Her stepfather (below) Dr Grimesby Roylott, who has a "violence of temper approaching mania" is the obvious suspect. When Roylott, who is so huge that his "hat . . . touched the top of the doorway" bursts in and threatens Holmes, it serves to heighten the tension of the situation and give "zest to our investigation".

Fotomas

"Sherlock Holmes (below) was transformed when he was hot upon a . . . scent . . . His face flushed and darkened. His brows were drawn into two hard, black lines, while his eyes shone out from beneath them with a steely glitter . . . His nostrils seemed to dilate with a purely animal lust for the chase". The tall, gaunt detective is passionate only about his work, steering clear of friendships, particularly those with women. Apart from Watson, he has no warm human contact, only clients. Solving criminal problems helps him to "escape from the common places of existence".

THE MAN WITH THE TWISTED LIP

"The sinister beggar who lives upon the second floor of the opium den" – the man with the twisted lip – is arrested for the murder of Neville St Clair. It is the fruit of his begging ("four hundred and twenty-one pennies, and two hundred and seventy half pennies") which has weighed down St Clair's coat – and perhaps St Clair himself – to the bottom of the Thames. The beggar is a well-known sight among City gents, one of whom, perhaps, was Neville St Clair himself, who commuted daily from his country home (left). He was "interested in several companies" – although the exact source of his income is a mystery.

THE BLUE CARBUNCLE

Henry Baker (left) is introduced via his "very seedy and disreputable hard felt hat", from which Sherlock Holmes deduces that he is "a man who leads a sedentary life, goes out little, is out of training entirely, is middle-aged, has grizzled hair which has been cut in the last few days, and which he anoints with lime". He also deduces that Baker is "highly intellectual" (because he has a large head), and that he was "well-to-do ... although he has now fallen upon evil days". When Baker arrives to retrieve his stolen goose, the deductions are shown to be true.

The "rat-faced" hotel attendant, James Ryder (right), proves to be an equally easy study for Holmes.

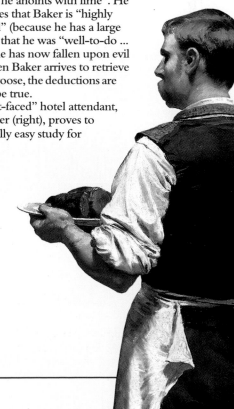

Mansell Collection

Fine Art Photographic Library

Fine Art Photographic Library (Both pictures)

MEN AND SUPERMEN

Unwilling to rest on the laurels of his great detective, Conan Doyle set himself to achieve greater literary status by inventing a gallery of unorthodox heroes, both honourable and eccentric.

According to Sir Arthur Conan Doyle, 'The first object of a novelist is to tell a tale'. Conan Doyle himself was a superb storyteller, whether he was writing detective novels or science fiction, historical romances, tales of the supernatural or histories of contemporary wars. But in his best work – above all in writing of Sherlock Holmes' adventures – Conan Doyle surpassed mere story-telling by creating unforgettable atmosphere as well as strong and unique characters. It is these qualities that make readers return again and again to the great detective's case-books long after the stories and solutions have become too familiar to hold any surprises.

By planting occasional, seemingly casual details in his narrative, Conan Doyle creates a powerful atmosphere. The details enable us to picture the comfortable, bachelor disorder of 221B Baker Street – and the more dangerous world outside.

BIRTH OF A SUPER-SLEUTH

The famous detective's methods owed a great deal to Conan Doyle's mentor, Dr Joseph Bell of Edinburgh, and also to Edgar Allan Poe's fictional French detective, Dupin, who used his powers of observation and deduction to solve the murders in the Rue Morgue. Holmes' mastery of disguise and his use of science to fight crime also have earlier parallels. But these aspects do not fully account for his appeal. Unlike earlier detectives, who served only as onlookers and solution-givers, Holmes plays a central, active role in his investigations. We are directed by his faithful biographer, Dr Watson, to concentrate more on the sleuth than on the victims or suspects involved in his case.

On the face of it, Holmes is the direct opposite of the warm-hearted, chivalrous, 'manly' Victorian hero. He is all intellect – a reasoning machine who lives only in his work. Sardonic and egocentric, he dislikes women and, Watson recalls, "never spoke of the softer passions, save with a gibe and a sneer". He rises late, unless he has stayed up all night. He never plays games and rarely takes exercise, though he somehow remains fit enough to take the most strenuous crises in his stride.

He is astonishingly ignorant of subjects such as astronomy and literature, which have

Awaiting patients
(Top) Arthur Conan Doyle as he was starting to make his name. He began his spectacularly successful writing career when he failed to make a living as a doctor.

A rare woman
(above) The beautiful actress Lola Montes was a model for Conan Doyle's fiction. She is thought to have inspired Irene Adler – the only woman to impress Sherlock Holmes.

First appearance
(above) The unforgettable Sherlock Holmes and Dr Watson were 'born' in 1887, in a story called A Study in Scarlet, *first published in Beeton's Christmas Annual.*

In the 'Strand'
(right) The fame of Conan Doyle and Sherlock Holmes spread worldwide when the Strand Magazine *commissioned a series of Holmes short stories.*

no bearing on his investigations, although his studies – including a monograph on the 140 known varieties of tobacco ash – are the last word in exhaustive scientific research.

Holmes' moral outlook seems, in Victorian terms, more than a little suspect. Without the stimulus of an unsolved crime he becomes bored, and injects himself with cocaine "as a protest against the monotony of existence". When confronted with the master criminal Professor Moriarty, he freely admits "My horror at his crimes was lost in admiration at his skill." And he has no qualms about taking the law into his own hands.

His tall, gaunt looks, subtle brain, bad habits and aesthetic love of music give him a passing resemblance to the villains rather than heroes of Victorian fiction – or at any rate to the 'decadents' of the 1890s. Yet, in reality, Holmes' unorthodoxy is largely sleight-of-hand on the part of Conan Doyle – Holmes is a gentleman and a model of rectitude. He works against the forces of evil. He may deplore the lack of imagination shown by the police, and enjoy deflating the bumptious Inspector Lestrade, but he generally allows the Force to take most of the credit for his successes. And he is patriotic, neatly drilling a bullet-hole pattern 'VR' (Victoria Regina) on the wall opposite his armchair. After Holmes' 'death' at the Reichenbach Falls, the honest Watson does not hesitate to call his friend "the best and the wisest man whom I have ever known".

An anti-social hero with a heart of gold appears again in the shape of another Conan Doyle original – Professor Challenger, "a primitive cave-man in a lounge suit", "a wild genius of a violent and intolerant disposition",

who "beats the world for offensiveness." Once again, his appeal was enormous to a Victorian readership who could pride themselves on seeing the worth of the man beneath his gruff exterior.

KILLING HIM OFF

Conan Doyle killed Holmes in 1893, after writing two novels and two collections of stories about him, because 'I have had such an overdose of him that I feel towards him as I do towards *pâté de foie gras*, of which I once ate too much, so that the name of it gives me a sickly feeling to this day.' Public protests and muni-

Scientific investigations
(above) Holmes' "profound" knowledge of chemistry reflects Conan Doyle's own medical training, as does the character Dr Watson. Holmes' interest is specific to his work: his knowledge of 'irrelevant' literature, for example, is "Nil".

ficent offers from magazines eventually persuaded Conan Doyle to write *The Hound of the Baskervilles* in 1902, said to be one of the dead detective's earlier cases. He was finally induced to bring Holmes back to life in the pages of *Strand Magazine*, with *The Empty House* (1903). After this, Conan Doyle became resigned to living with his creation, and by the time of his death there were no less than 60 Sherlock Holmes cases on record, four in the form of novels.

HISTORICAL NOVELS

Another of Conan Doyle's objections to Holmes was that 'he takes my mind from better things'. Conan Doyle believed that his historical novels were his most important contributions to literature. He carried out an immense amount of research on English and French history, and wrote the novels fast and furiously. He boasted that he had written 10,000 words of *The Refugees* in 24 hours, and he worked a 15-hour day on his medieval romance, *The White Company*. This was the novel he most enjoyed writing, and he noted that on finishing 'I felt a wave of exultation and with a cry of "That's done it!" I hurled my inky pen across the room . . . I knew in my heart that the book would live and that it would illuminate our national traditions.'

Conan Doyle was mistaken. The historical novels are very readable as adventure stories, and one expert considers them to be amongst the finest historical novels of the late 19th century. But they are not great classics. There is far more of his characteristic vigour and humour in the various *Exploits* (1895) and

"IDÉAL·BIBLIOTHÈQUE"
L'Ouvrage complet : 2 francs.

CONAN DOYLE

LA GRANDE OMBRE

ÉDITIONS PIERRE LAFITTE

SIR NIGEL
is the hero of Sir A. Conan Doyle's stirring new serial which commences in the December Xmas Double Number of the "Strand Magazine." The above picture illustrates a thrilling incident in the first instalment.
STRAND MAGAZINE

Medieval chivalry *(left) Military adventure, chivalry and 'team-spirit' feature highly in the medieval romance* Sir Nigel. *Published in 1906, it recounts the early life of Sir Nigel, hero of* The White Company, *written 15 years previously. Conan Doyle was disappointed by its muted reception.*

Napoleonic France *(above) More recent French history proved a potent source of inspiration. The Great Shadow (shown here in French translation) contains a vivid account of the Battle of Waterloo. But the author's most popular French stories are those about the comic Napoleonic hero Brigadier Gerard.*

Adventures (1905) of the swashbuckling Napoleonic veteran, Brigadier Gerard – a creation, like Holmes, that Doyle underrated. Some aspects of his character were probably suggested by Doyle's one-time friend, the eccentric Dr Budd, who may also have been the model for Professor Challenger.

The Lost World (1912), the other Challenger stories, and his last work of fiction, *The Maracot Deep* (1929) show Conan Doyle continuing to break new ground. From early beginnings as a struggling, unsuccessful doctor until the end of his life, his flair for creating larger-than-life characters and gripping tales remained undiminished.

The tall, gaunt Sherlock Holmes and his friend Dr John Watson entered the hearts and imaginations of the British public. So enduring was their hold that Conan Doyle was compelled to devise more and more adventures for his heroes.

He attempted to dispose of Holmes in the *Memoirs of Sherlock Holmes* (1894), having grown tired of his too-popular creation, but his readers would not allow it. Conan Doyle consequently went on to write *The Hound of the Baskervilles* (1902) and numerous other tales about the master sleuth. The characters evolved with the years as their creator turned increasingly to psychological problems rather than straight detection.

Although these are by far his most famous works, Conan Doyle also wrote some stirring historical novels, notably *The White Company* (1891) and *Rodney Stone* (1896), while his knowledge of Napoleonic France was put to entertaining effect in *The Exploits of Brigadier Gerard* (1895).

Conan Doyle was finally drawn to science fiction, producing a classic story in *The Lost World* (1912).

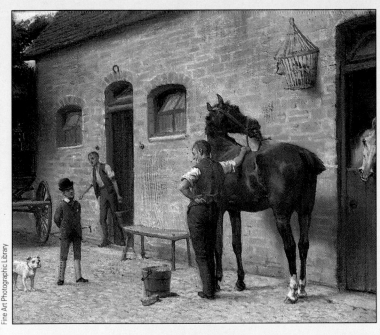

Fine Art Photographic Library

THE MEMOIRS OF SHERLOCK HOLMES

◆ 1894 ◆

The disappearance of the racehorse, Silver Blaze (above), and the murder of its trainer, John Straker, present the first challenge to Sherlock Holmes in his *Memoirs*. The horse was favourite for the Wessex Cup and consequently the case was "the one topic of conversation through the length and breadth of England". When Holmes investigates at the stables on Dartmoor, he quickly discovers that Straker was not quite the man he pretended to be, and that there is only one possible place in which Silver Blaze can be concealed. But with a typically dramatic flourish, he reveals everything only after an apparently unknown horse has carried off the Wessex Cup.

Conan Doyle said himself that in 'Silver Blaze' his ignorance about flat racing was blatantly obvious. But whatever minor flaws there may be in accuracy of detail, they pale in comparison to the masterful handling of facts and deductions, and the skill with which the reader is gripped from beginning to end of the story.

Apart from the 'Adventure of Silver Blaze', the other stories include Holmes' very first case, and also the investigation that first made his name, in which he solves the riddle of the ancient Musgrave Ritual. 'The Final Problem' introduces us to Holmes' arch-enemy, Professor Moriarty, "the Napoleon of crime", whose vast organization Holmes destroys. But Moriarty escapes, and, bent on revenge, pursues Holmes and Watson across the continent. At the Reichenbach Falls in Switzerland, Watson is lured away and the masterminds of crime and detection engage in a final, fatal duel (right).

The eleven adventures in *The Memoirs of Sherlock Holmes* were intended to make up Conan Doyle's last book about his famous sleuth. But he had not anticipated the strength of the public's affection for and commitment to Holmes – their hero was not allowed to die.

Mansell Collection

THE HOUND OF THE BASKERVILLES

◆ 1902 ◆

A gigantic hound (right) is the chief suspect in a murder hunt. Its footprints are found beside the body of Sir Charles Baskerville, recently found dead, with 'strangely distorted features', on the moors close to his Devonshire mansion (right). Dr Mortimer, who relates these details to Holmes and Watson, more than half believes the legend that makes a supernatural hound the appointed doom of the Baskerville family. He persuades Holmes to meet Sir Henry, the last of the Baskervilles, who has returned from Canada to claim his inheritance. The strange theft of one of Sir Henry's boots, and the activities of an elusive spy, suggest that Sir Henry is indeed in danger. Watson accompanies Sir Henry to Baskerville Hall, where he encounters shifty servants, an escaped convict, and various neighbours including the naturalist Stapleton, with whose sister Sir Henry falls in love. However, the most likely suspect, a mysterious stranger, turns out to be none other than Holmes himself in disguise. Holmes' investigations reveal Sir Charles' murderer, and Holmes sets a trap for him on the moors, using Sir Henry as the bait. At the climax, the mystery of the gigantic hound is explained, and the treacherous, fog-wreathed Grimpen Mire claims another victim.

Fine Art Photographic Library

THE WHITE COMPANY

◆ 1891 ◆

(Left) Alleyne Edricson's love for the beautiful Maude, daughter of Sir Nigel Loring, is one of the key incidents in this romance of medieval chivalry. Unless he succeeds in recovering his ancestral manor from his elder brother, Alleyne cannot hope that Sir Nigel will consent to the match; but at least he can prove himself worthy of Maude by performing great deeds in the French wars. With him go two old acquaintances – the burly, boisterous Hordle John and the veteran archer Sam Aylward. The three companions-in-arms take service in the White Company led by Sir Nigel, going through an encounter with pirates, a testing siege and a bloody battle before their destinies are decided. This panorama of 14th-century society contains a host of characters and places. It was the book that Conan Doyle most enjoyed writing: 'I was young and full of the first joy of life and action and I think I got some of it into my pages.'

RODNEY STONE

◆ 1896 ◆

The bare-knuckle fight between Champion Harrison (right) and Crab Wilson is the high point of this exciting Regency novel, in which wild aristocratic 'bucks' ruin themselves at cards, take part in reckless races, and act as patrons and sponsors of prize-fighting. At a meeting of 'the Fancy' – the prize-fighting fraternity – Rodney Stone's great friend, Boy Jim, turns up and issues a general challenge. The nephew of a once-famous fighter, Champion Harrison, he has determined to make his way by the same means. He proves his ability and is matched against Crab Wilson, a pugilist backed by the villainous Sir Lothian Hume. But on the day of the fight Boy Jim fails to appear, and his place is taken by Champion Harrison. A mighty battle ensues. After its unexpected outcome, Rodney and his uncle Sir Charles Tregellis are summoned to Cliffe Royal, a house at which a notorious murder has occurred 14 years earlier. There Boy Jim accounts for his non-appearance, a new explanation of the murder is given, and Sir Lothian receives his just deserts.

D. Maclise: Pugalist/Forbes Magazine Collection/Bridgeman Art Library

Fine Art Photographic Library

THE EXPLOITS OF BRIGADIER GERARD

✦ 1896 ✦

Boastful and brave, a gallant lady's-man, Brigadier Gerard (right) is one of Conan Doyle's most endearing creations. A hussar officer in Napoleon's campaigns, he tells of his many exploits, remaining sublimely unconscious of his frequent blunders. Napoleon says of him that if he "has the thickest head he has also the stoutest heart in my army." In a typical story, he tears himself away from his amours to second Napoleon in a duel of honour. To his horror, he sees the little Emperor run through and killed. Though he exacts a fearless revenge on the Sicilian murderers, Gerard's fortunes seem, for a time, irredeemable.

Fine Art Photographic Library

THE LOST WORLD

✦ 1912 ✦

Prehistoric creatures roam the 'lost world' of Amazonia (left), or so the outrageously irascible, big-bearded Professor Challenger claims. When he organizes an expedition to try to prove his story, he is joined by his staunchest scholarly opponent, Professor Summerlee, the explorer John Roxton and the journalist Edward Dunn Malone. Malone is the narrator, whose main objective in going along is to impress the girl he loves. After several days' march into the interior of Amazonia, the companions reach the base of a high plateau, entirely cut off from the swamp land beneath it. There they see their first pterodactyl, and it soon becomes evident that Challenger has, in truth, discovered a prehistoric world of titanic reptiles. Then the party stumble across human and near-human beings – Indians and the ape-men who terrorize them. They help the Indians to victory, and thanks to Challenger, the four men manage to leave the plateau by balloon, returning eventually to London and a suitably triumphant reception.

Elementary Detection

Investigative techniques were in their infancy in the Victorian era, but the advent of photography and forensic science gave the law enforcers a fighting chance.

Sherlock Holmes made his fictional debut in *A Study in Scarlet* in 1887; a year later the gruesome Jack the Ripper murders horrified London. There could scarcely be a greater contrast than that between the brilliant investigative feats of the hawk-eyed detective and the bungling attempts of his real-life counterparts to find the savage killer.

The failure to capture the Ripper caused widespread resentment against the police, with protests coming not only from the squalid East End of the capital where the murders were committed, but also from the highest in the land. Some of the more politely worded rebukes came from Queen Victoria herself, who took a keen interest in the case and felt that 'the detective department is not as efficient as it might be'. Others were less tactful, with the satirical magazine *Punch* poking fun at 'the Defective Department'.

Law enforcement as we know it had begun in 1829, when Robert Peel, then Home Secretary, had pushed through the Metropolitan Police Act, creating London's first disciplined police force. Since Peel thought that 'the primary function of an efficient police is the *prevention* of crime', his force consisted mainly of uniformed officers patrolling the streets. While the 'Peelers' were not recruited primarily for their brilliance or education (some could not even read), the Metropolitan Police did set high standards in other ways. And, after initially arousing suspicion and hostility, they gained an enviable reputation for courage and fair play. The degree of public acceptance and administration was clearly shown in 1872, when a threatened police strike was met with newspaper pleas to the force not to abandon the streets to criminals.

GOING UNDERCOVER

In 1842 a small Detective Department consisting of two inspectors and six sergeants was set up, though not everyone approved of the idea. The critics were wary of the growth of underhand 'continental' espionage methods which had come to light in the infamous 1833 Popay case. William Popay, a police sergeant, had passed himself off as a poor artist to infiltrate a subversive movement. When the public found out about Popay's underhand methods, there was an outcry. The police dismissed him. British resistance to an undercover police service was so deeply ingrained that in 1869 the Commissioner of Police reported that a detective system was 'viewed with the greatest suspicion . . . by the majority of Englishmen and is, in fact, entirely

A sea chase
Thinly disguised as father and son, Hawley Crippen and his lover Ethel le Neve were apprehended on board the SS Monrose when it docked near Quebec. The case made history – it was the first time that a wireless had been used to transmit a vital message across the water. The ensuing sea chase made Chief Inspector Dew into a national hero.

Police through the ages
The 1750s saw the establishment of the Bow Street Runners (above left), early law enforcers who patrolled the streets of London. One hundred years later Victorian 'Peelers' (left) wore top hats and full uniform, and indeed were respected as much for their uniform as for the duties they performed. The rare attempts by some officers at going undercover were viewed as contemptible – foreign tactics at their worst. Today's Metropolitan Police force was founded in 1829 and the turn-of-the-century scene (above) shows one officer peacefully directing traffic.

foreign to the habits and feelings of the nation'. At this time, there were only 15 detectives in the Metropolitan Police out of a force of 8000.

There were some prominent supporters of the new Detective Department. Charles Dickens considered that it was 'so well-chosen and trained, proceeds so systematically and quietly, does its business in such a workmanlike manner and is always so steadily engaged in the service of the public, that the public really do not know enough of it, to know a tithe of its usefulness.' (Dickens was the first writer to create a fictional detective from the Metropolitan Police – Inspector Bucket in *Bleak House* published 1852-53.)

The picture painted by Dickens was certainly too rosy, for in 1877 three of the four Chief Inspectors in the Department were found guilty of corruption. This prompted a Home Office inquiry and, in 1878, the creation of the newly organized Criminal Investigation Department (CID). There were initially about 250 men attached to the department, but 10 years later, when Jack the Ripper had his brief reign of terror, the number had risen to approximately 800.

Between August and November 1888, Jack the Ripper killed and mutilated five East End prostitutes. While brutal crime was no novelty in this area, these five killings won unprecedented publicity because of their savagery. The public responded with various tip-offs, leading to more than 100 arrests, but the search was hampered because the police had too fixed an idea about the nature of the killer. Anyone 'respectable' (which meant nothing more significant than that they had a decent address) was immediately removed from the list of potential suspects.

The Commissioner of the Metropolitan Police, Sir Charles Warren, handled the case so ineptly that he had to resign even before the final murder was committed. His most incompetent act was to wipe off the murderer's message – chalked on a wall near one of the murder sites – before it could be photographed. His justification for destroying this vital clue was that he was afraid the anti-semitic message would incite trouble in an area with a large Jewish population. Warren also put his faith in a pair of prize bloodhounds – Burgho and Barnaby – who merely succeeded in tracking down entirely innocent people, including a plain-clothes policeman.

Extraordinary means were employed for identifying or trapping the killer. The eyes of one of the victims were photographed in the then popular belief that the last thing they had seen would be imprinted on their eyes. It was even suggested that young, clean-shaven boxers should be disguised as prostitutes to roam the streets at night, wearing steel collars to protect their necks from the Ripper's knife.

The *Sherlock Holmes* stories reinforced the public's image of an inefficient detective force, for Conan Doyle invariably depicts the plodders from the Yard hopelessly trailing several steps behind his crime-solving genius. Fortunately for the police, most of the serious crimes which they had tackled until then had been much less baffling than the Ripper case itself or those solved by Holmes.

For then, as now, most murders were committed either by a relative or associate of the victim, or in the course of another crime (such as a robbery) by someone who already had a criminal record, and whose habits and haunts were well-known to the police. Such crimes were more often solved by patience than by extraordinary mental agility.

In their fight against crime, the Victorian police had few of the aids that are taken for granted today. Foren-

Mary Evans Picture Library

Fingerprints
Although viewed with a mixture of suspicion and derision at the time, the advent of fingerprinting heralded a vast leap forward for crime detection.

Scotland Yard's Photo Lab
(left) Used to record evidence at the scene of the crime, photography proved to be one more tool in the drive for law enforcement. This first photographic department at New Scotland Yard dates back to 1905.

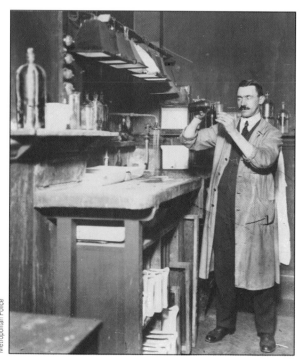

Metropolitan Police

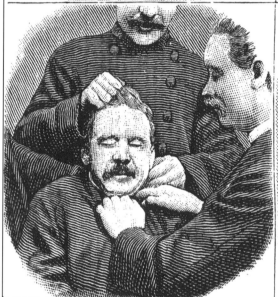

Captured on film
(above) Some forces had a 'Rogues Gallery' – walls plastered with mugshots of suspects. But few prisoners submitted willingly to this, and the likenesses could be deceptive.

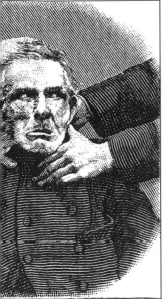

sic science had been used as long ago as 1786, when police trapped a murderer in Kirkcudbrightshire, Scotland by taking plaster casts of his footprints. But forensics had advanced little since then. Consequently, the police were about 10 years behind Sherlock Holmes who, when first introduced to Dr Watson, is overjoyed because he has just discovered an infallible test for identifying bloodstains – "the most practical medico-legal discovery for years." In real life, the biochemical analysis of blood in crime detection was not used until the early 20th century.

Fingerprinting was also introduced in the early 1900s. The idea was brought to England by Sir Edward Henry, who had been Inspector-General of Police in Bengal, where thumb-prints were used to identify illiterate workers. When he became head of the CID in 1901, Henry immediately established Scotland Yard's fingerprint section.

At first there was great resistance to this new-fangled idea, as displayed by a 'disgusted' magistrate who wrote to a national newspaper: 'Scotland Yard, once known as the world's finest police organization, will be the laughing-stock of Europe if it insists on trying to trace criminals by odd ridges on their skins. I, for one, am firmly convinced that no British jury will ever convict a man on "evidence" produced by the half-baked theories some official happened to pick up in India.'

Four years later, however, fingerprint evidence was first used to obtain a murder conviction, when the brothers Alfred and Albert Stratton were found guilty of killing an elderly couple while robbing their shop. Alfred Stratton had left a bloody thumb-print on a cash box, and his defending counsel's contention that the fingerprint system was 'unreliable' and 'savoured more of the French courts than of English justice' was to no avail. The brothers were hanged.

Before the introduction of fingerprinting, criminals had been identified by means of photographs and records, but the system was highly fallible. Eddie

Guerin, a French-Irish-American gangster, wrote in his memoirs (1928) that 'on my way to the photographer I picked up a couple of pebbles, put them in my mouth, and screwed up my face until even my own mother would not have recognized me.' The Criminal Records Office (established in 1871) was so inefficient that convicted criminals could beat the system simply by assuming aliases once they had been released from prison.

OUTWITTING THE POLICE

This tactic was used by Charlie Peace, one of the most notorious of Victorian criminals, to try to evade the hangman. Fleeing from Sheffield in 1876, after murdering the husband of a woman with whom he was having an affair, Peace settled in London. He shaved off his beard, dyed his hair, changed his appearance and continued his successful career as a cat burglar. But in 1878, having shot a policeman who caught him breaking into a house, he was captured, tried under his assumed name of John Ward and sentenced to life imprisonment. Unfortunately for him, his current lover decided to claim the £100 reward money for identifying him. Peace was therefore retried under his real name, found guilty in 1879 and sentenced to death by hanging.

The Peace case clearly illustrates the rudimentary communications between regional police forces, of which there were more than 200 in England by the end of the 19th century. The police travelled by public transport, reports were handwritten, and Scotland Yard did not even have a telephone until 1901. With the establishment of a detective training school in 1902, professional standards began to improve at the Yard. But when Scotland Yard detectives were called to help regional police, they often found that they were contending with amateurish police methods as well as with the criminal.

In 1908, for example, Chief Inspector Walter Dew (who had worked on the Jack the Ripper case and later

On the beat
All constables were armed with truncheons, although the Rural Constabulary Act of 1839 permitted the issue of cutlasses. By the 1880s, however, night patrolmen could request revolvers.

Reign of Terror
Jack the Ripper was infamous for his savagery. Not content with simply murdering his victims, he would gut their entrails, dismember them and send specimens to the police.

became famous when he arrested Dr Crippen) investigated the murder of a 12-year-old boy in Salisbury, Wiltshire. When he arrived the day after the killing, he was dismayed to find that the local police had allowed the boy's family to clean up the scene of the crime and have the corpse washed. Dew charged the boy's mother with the murder, but after two trials (the jury in the first were unable to agree on a verdict) she was acquitted.

Chief Inspector Dew was a member of the CID's 'Murder Squad' (never an official title), founded in 1907 to solve difficult murder cases. The Squad made its mark by solving the Dr Crippen case, although flawed investigative techniques nearly enabled Crippen to get off scot-free.

Hawley Harvey Crippen was an American who had settled in England in 1900, with his second wife Cora. Ten years later he poisoned her, cut her up and buried parts of the body in the cellar of his house. A few weeks after the murder, his secretary and lover, Ethel le Neve, moved in with him. Friends, worried about Cora's disappearance, alerted Scotland Yard who sent down Chief Inspector Dew. He interviewed Crippen and searched the house but found nothing suspicious.

A RACE ACROSS THE OCEAN

Crippen, who had told friends that Cora had returned to America and died there, now changed his story. He told Dew that she had left him and that he had invented her death to save face. If Crippen's nerve had held he would have probably got away with it, but he panicked and ran. By the time Dew returned three days later to check a routine point, Crippen and Ethel were fleeing across the Channel. Two days later the remains of Cora Crippen were dug up.

Descriptions of the wanted couple were circulated, and Captain Kendall of the *SS Monrose*, sailing from Antwerp to Canada, thought that he recognized them among his passengers – ineptly disguised as father and son. He sent a wireless message to Dew, who sailed from Liverpool in a faster ship, arriving near Quebec two days before the pair of suspects. They were taken straight back to England where Crippen was found guilty and hanged, and Ethel was acquitted. What made the case so famous was the drama of the sea chase and the fact that a wireless had been used for the first time to catch a murderer. People in England had read about Dew's pursuit – while the fugitives were blissfully unaware that they were being followed. Dew was lionized in the press, and the detective's image was transformed from half-wit to hero.

But Dew's handling of the initial investigation left much to be desired. It had never occurred to him, for example, to ask Crippen why his wife had left behind her expensive collection of dresses if, as he alleged, she had returned permanently to America. And if he had taken the precaution of having Crippen watched, he would never have been able to escape. Sherlock Holmes would never have slipped up in this way. But Conan Doyle could not have bettered the perfect irony of the unsuspecting Crippen, just days away from Canada and freedom, looking at the ship's crackling wireless aerial and remarking, 'What a wonderful invention it is!'

Two faces of the law
The popular image of the police in Victorian times was not simply one of men unswervingly pursuing the guilty, regardless of race, creed or background. All too often the aristocracy was treated with kid gloves, no matter what their crime, while the working classes were subjected to a much more violent enactment of 'justice'. And in the course of duty, police were liable to commit acts of folly and ineptitude – and, at times, even be guilty of corruption.

BIBLIOGRAPHY

Ashley, R., *Wilkie Collins*. Haskell Booksellers (Brooklyn, 1975)

Berenbaum, Linda B., *The Gothic Imagination: Expansion in Gothic Literature and Art*. Fairleigh Dickinson University Press (East Brunswick, 1981)

Browne, W. A., *What Asylums Were, Are and Ought to Be: Being the Substance of Five Lectures Delivered Before the Managers of the Montrose Royal Lunatic Asylum* (reprint). Ayer Co. Publications (Salem, 1976)

Buchholz, Heinrich E., *Edgar Allan Poe: A Centenary Tribute* (reprint of 1910 edition). Arden Library (Darby, 1978)

Cameron, Kenneth N., *Shelley: The Golden Years*. Harvard University Press (Cambridge, 1974)

Church, Richard, *Mary Shelley* (reprint of 1928 edition). Arden Library (Darby, 1978)

Clairmont, Claire, *The Journals of Claire Clairmont*. Harvard University Press (Cambridge, 1968)

Cline, C., *Byron, Shelley and Their Pisan Circle*. Richard West (Philadelphia, 1952)

Clough, E. R., *A Study of Mary Wollstonecraft and the Rights of Women*. Gordon Press (New York, 1972)

Cox, Don R., *Arthur Conan Doyle*. Ungar, Frederick (New York, 1985)

Dawson, P.M., *The Unacknowledged Legislator: Shelley and Politics*. Oxford University Press (New York, 1980)

Day, William P., *In the Circle of Fear and Desire: A Study of Gothic Fantasy*. University of Chicago Press (Chicago, 1985)

Didier, E. L., *Life and Poems of Edgar Allan Poe*. Haskell Booksellers (Brooklyn, 1974)

Dunn, Jane, *Moon in Eclipse: A Life of Mary Shelley*. St Martin's Press (New York, 1978)

Edwards, Owen, *The Quest for Sherlock Holmes*. State Mutual Book and Periodical Service (New York, 1981)

Ellis, Stewart M., *Wilkie Collins, le Fanu and Others* (reprint of 1931 edition). Richard West (Philadelphia, 1973)

Fruit, John P., *The Mind and Art of Poe's Poetry* (reprint of 1899 edition). Arden Library (Darby, 1980)

Glut, Donald F., *The Frankenstein Legend: A Tribute to Mary Shelley and Boris Karloff*. Scarecrow Press (Metuchen, 1973)

Hood, George S., *Edgar Allan Poe* (reprint of 1897 edition). Folcroft (Folcroft, 1972)

James, D. G., *Byron and Shelley*. Folcroft (Folcroft, 1951)

Keiley, Jarvis, *Edgar Allan Poe*. Haskell Booksellers (Brooklyn, 1974)

Lachtman, Howard, *Sherlock Slept Here: Conan Doyle's Travels in America*. Capra Press (Santa Barbara, 1985)

Locke, Don, *A Fantasy of Reason: The Life and Thought of William Godwin*. Routledge & Kegan Paul (Boston, 1980)

Nakamura, Junichi, *Edgar Allan Poe's Relations with New England*. Darby Books (Darby, 1981)

Page, Norman, ed., *Wilkie Collins: The Critical Heritage*. Routledge & Kegan Paul (Boston, 1974)

Pearson, Hesketh, *Conan Doyle: His Life and Art*. Taplinger (New York, 1977)

Pope-Hennessy, Una, *Edgar Allan Poe* (reprint of 1934 edition). Haskell Booksellers (Brooklyn, 1969)

Powers, Katherine R., *The Influence of William Godwin on the Novels of Mary Shelley*. Ayer Co. Publications (Salem, 1980)

Robinson, Kenneth, *Wilkie Collins, a Biography* (reprint of 1951 edition). Greenwood Press (Westport, 1973)

Robinson, Victor, *William Godwin and Mary Wollstonecraft: Lives of Great Altrurians*. Folcroft (Folcroft, 1978)

Sayers, Dorothy L., *Wilkie Collins, a Critical and Biographical Study*. Friends of the University of Toledo Libraries (Toledo, 1977)

Starrett, V., *Private Life of Sherlock Holmes* (reprint of 1934 edition). Haskell Booksellers (Brooklyn, 1970)

Symons, Julian, *The Tell-Tale Heart: The Life and Works of Edgar Allan Poe*. Harper & Row (New York, 1978)

Vasbinder, Samuel H., *Scientific Attitudes in Mary Shelley's Frankenstein*. UMI Research Press (Ann Arbor, 1984)

Wilkes, John, *The London Police in the Nineteenth Century*. Lerner Publications (Minneapolis, 1984)

Wollstonecraft, Mary, *The Love Letters of Mary Wollstonecraft to Gilbert Imlay* (reprint of 1908 edition). Folcroft (Folcroft, 1974)

INDEX